Pink Ribbon Quilts

A BOOK BECAUSE OF BREAST CANCER

Mimi Dietrich

Martingale
& COMPANY

BOTHELL, WASHINGTON

Acknowledgments

EACH QUILTER THAT worked on a quilt was very enthusiastic about the project. They all wanted, in a quilter's special way, to make a contribution toward the fight against breast cancer. Many of the quilters have been touched personally by breast cancer. Their mothers, sisters, daughters, or friends have had the disease. One quilt was made by a group of five quilters who are survivors. I think the bravest quilter is a friend who worked on a quilt one night and told us her daughter was going through tests. But we all laughed and cried and worked together and tried our best to be hopeful. We want to make a difference.

Many thanks to:

URSULA REIKES AND the staff at Martingale & Company for their enthusiasm and support of this project; The Gertrudes for stitching Rosebuds for Recovery; Monday Night Madness for stitching Buttons and Bows; the Catonsville Quilt and Tea Society for piecing ribbons; the Graduate Class for appliquéing and piecing ribbons; the Friendship Quilters in Linthicum, Maryland, for making Broken Dishes blocks; The Great American Quilters for making the raffle quilt; Village Quilters in Catonsville for making blocks five years ago; the staff at Seminole Sampler for arranging fabrics in the heart; Norma Campbell for sharing her friendship; Karen Trent, M.D, and Julia Blum, M.D., for sharing their talents; Mary Rutter, R.N., for sharing her thoughts as an oncology nurse; Regina English for sharing her words of wisdom; Patti Muller for sharing her words of experience; Carol Doak, for designing the paper-pieced ribbon; she's the expert! Karan Flanscha for researching flower symbolism; Barbara Jacobson for her stitches; Mary Hickey for sending her new fabric with pink ribbons; Bonnie Benn Stratton for "Quilt for a Cure™" fabrics; Robbyn Robinson for helping me find so many nice color combinations to go with pink; Nicki Becker for introducing me to the easy fusible method of making watercolor quilts; Linda Newsom for her reliable machine quilting; Sandy Pfau for her openness; Dave Hammond for my new author photo; Laurie Gregg for her friendship; and Bob Dietrich for his never-ending patience.

Credits

President . . . . Nancy J. Martin
CEO/Publisher . . . . Daniel J. Martin
Associate Publisher . . . . Jane Hamada
Editorial Director . . . . Mary V. Green
Design and Production Manager . . . . Cheryl Stevenson
Technical Editor . . . . Ursula Reikes
Copy Editor . . . . Liz McGehee
Illustrator . . . . Robin Strobel
Photographer . . . . Brent Kane
Designer . . . . Trina Stahl

Pink Ribbon Quilts: A Book Because of Breast Cancer
© 1999 by Mimi Dietrich

Martingale & Company
PO Box 118
Bothell, WA 98041-0118 USA
www.patchwork.com

Printed in Canada
04 03 02 6 5 4 3

That Patchwork Place is an imprint of Martingale & Company.

Mission Statement

We are dedicated to providing quality products and service by working together to inspire creativity and to enrich the lives we touch.

Library of Congress Cataloging-in-Publication Data
Dietrich, Mimi.
    Pink ribbon quilts : a book because of breast cancer / Mimi Dietrich.
        p.   cm.
    ISBN 1-56477-279-9
    1. Patchwork Patterns.   2. Quilting Patterns.   3. Breast—Cancer.
I. Title
TT835.D544   1999
746.46'041—dc21   99-40527
                                                    CIP

Contents

Introduction

FIVE YEARS AGO, I was diagnosed with breast cancer after a mammogram showed a "suspicious spot." I then had a lumpectomy, followed by six weeks of radiation—and I lived!

This book is a celebration of my experience. It is dedicated to my family, whom I treasure more than ever, and to the wonderful doctors I have visited in the past five years. It is especially dedicated to my quilting friends, who helped me get through some tough days and taught me so much about the value of friendship.

Ten years ago, this book would not have been possible. Breast cancer was not something to talk about. But in 1992, a student in my year-long quilting class had surgery. She came to class to be with us even though she could not do her homework. She shared her experiences as her show-and-tell. Her openness taught us to overcome our fears and become aware of the effects of breast cancer.

Her positive attitude was terrific. She was a great help when I had to go through treatments. You learn much more than quilting in a quilting class!

One of the most overwhelming experiences I had was the day I visited the oncologist for the first time. I took my *Quilter's Newsletter Magazine* with me because I knew I would have to wait and I just needed to look at pictures and read short articles. When I met the oncologist, the first thing she said was "I get that magazine." Wow! I was at ease immediately—what could be better than a doctor who knows about quilts? It made me wonder if God is a quilter!

Quilting played a very important part in my positive attitude and recovery. I had just signed a contract with That Patchwork Place to write a book about the quilts at the Smithsonian. I could have given up the project. Instead, my doctor encouraged me to do it. I researched and planned designs, worked on quilts, shopped for fabric, and always tried to look forward. On one memorable day, I visited the oncologist in the morning and went to the museum to view spectacular quilts in the afternoon. In between I rested—I had to.

Many friends and students asked if they could do something to help. I remember being shocked and overwhelmed when friends at the local quilt shop would offer to grocery shop for me. It took me awhile to realize that friends just needed to do something for me. Since my family was already great about doing the grocery shopping, I printed a pattern for a quilt I needed for the new book. The original museum quilt was a friendship quilt made in Maryland, so I asked friends and students to make a block instead of sending a card. It was fabulous to receive the blocks one at a time in the mail. I hung them on a clothesline in my sewing room and enjoyed them until I felt well enough to sew them together.

A group of friends gave me a bear with a Band-Aid (strategically placed!). The bear has a little quilt with hearts and the signatures of my friends. The quilt may be small, but it is a special reminder of the value of friendship.

My quilt group, the Village Quilters, gave me a wonderful box of signed patchwork blocks. It was heartwarming to read each

name as I set the blocks together and pieced the quilt top. I added fabric with pink ribbons to complete this special breast-cancer quilt (photo below).

I think quilting is wonderful for all of us because it sparks our creativity, gives us goals, focuses our attention on positive projects, and brings us together with other quilters. Quilters all understand the simple thrill of finding just the right fabric on a shopping spree or sharing a fat quarter with another quilter.

If I mention my experience during a lecture or workshop, there is always a woman who walks up to me and shares her adventures as a survivor of breast cancer. It is amazing how many quilters are touched by this disease.

I write these experiences for you because I want all quilters to know how important their talents are. Quilt pieces may be small, but when they are stitched together with love and friendship, they can be very powerful. They make tears turn to smiles. They speak of hope and caring. They wrap us in love and remind us how precious life is.

If you know someone who has been touched by breast cancer, take some fabric and start to make her a quilt block. When your friend receives it, she will smile and feel better immediately. Or, gather some quilters together and make a quilt to raise money for breast-cancer research. You will smile, too, knowing that you have done something very special.

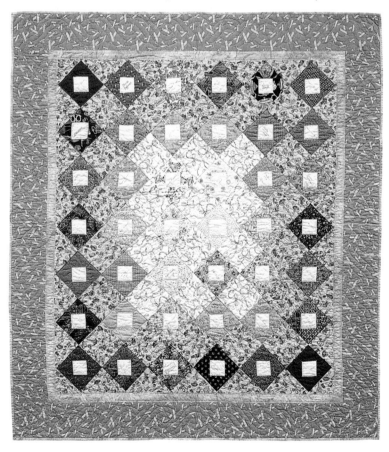

Pink Ribbons and Quilting Angels from the Village Quilters, 1994, Catonsville, Maryland, 48" x 55", quilted by Mimi Dietrich, 1995.

*Love,
Mimi*

The Quilts

QUILTS REMIND US of warmth, comfort, and love. What better way to show you care than to wrap a breast-cancer patient in a specially made quilt!

Among the projects in this book are small quilts that friends can make for the patient. You'll also find block ideas for group quilts and family quilts. There is even a full-sized raffle quilt you can make to raise money for breast-cancer organizations. Or, the patient may want to make one of the small quilts specially included to thank her caregivers.

All the quilts in this book have pink ribbons or pink fabric in the design. Pink ribbons are symbols of breast-cancer awareness. They remind us to get our mammograms and fight breast cancer through early detection. Quick-and-easy techniques and traditional blocks mean the small quilts can be finished quickly. If you like, the small quilts can be made larger by simply sewing more blocks, lengthening the borders, and of course, purchasing extra fabric.

Most of the quilts were machine quilted rather than hand quilted. If you are making a quilt for a sick friend, you'll want to complete the quilt quickly before she gets better. Your friend will appreciate a finished quilt and love cuddling up in it or laying it over her bed. With machine quilting, you can complete a small quilt in a few hours.

Fabric

ALL THE QUILTS in this book are made with fabrics with an "attitude"—a bright, cheerful, and positive attitude! The colors and prints are appropriate for the cheerful intentions of the projects. Some of the fabrics have ribbon prints to symbolize breast-cancer awareness, or flowers for love and good thoughts. The cream fabric in the "Woven Ribbons" quilt (page 23) and pillow is printed with butterflies, a symbol of hope and life. The white fabric used in "Buttons and Bows" (page 29) has little white buttons printed on the white fabric. They may be difficult to see in the photograph, but we could see them as we sewed, and it made each little square fun to stitch.

If you are making a quilt for a special person, consider using a fabric with her favorite print or color. Shopping for the perfect fabric can be as much fun as making the quilts. When you are in a quilt shop, look for fabrics marked "Quilt for a Cure." A portion of the purchase price of these fabrics is donated to breast-cancer research.

All the fabrics used in the quilts are 100% cotton. Prewash all fabrics to prevent shrinking and bleeding in the quilt. Wash dark and light colors separately with laundry detergent so that the dark colors do not run onto the light colors. Sometimes it is necessary to rinse dark fabrics a few times until the color stops bleeding and the rinse water is clear. Iron the fabrics so that the pieces will be accurate when you cut them.

Pink is used in each of the quilts because pink is the color used for ribbons representing breast-cancer awareness. Most of the quilts have a design element that looks like a pink ribbon. In many of the quilts, the inner border is made of pink fabric to symbolize the pink ribbons. There are appliquéd ribbons and paper-pieced ribbons, but most of the quilts have a more subtle way of speaking about breast cancer. The pink "Rosebuds for Recovery" (page 49) look to a budding new outlook on life after someone has had cancer. The dark pink shapes on the "Blossoms of Hope" are tears that have been shed because we are scared or because someone has been lost to the disease. The dogwood flowers symbolize "love in adversity" and "durability."

You can combine pink with purple, blue, green, or a complete spectrum of colors to create a quilt with a special message.

"Quilt for a Cure" fabrics

WRITING ON FABRIC

IT'S FUN AND easy to add a personal touch by writing on fabric. Keep these hints in mind.

- ✦ Iron a strip of freezer paper to the wrong side of the fabric. This will stabilize the fabric while you are writing. You can also place a piece of masking tape on the wrong side.

- ✦ Write your message on a computer and print it out. Tape the message to a light box or window. Tape the fabric on top of the message. Trace the message on the fabric using a Pigma 01 fine-line permanent pen.

- ✦ To get the thick and thin look of printed letters, trace the letters twice and fill in some areas.

- ✦ Of course, your own handwriting adds a very personal touch.

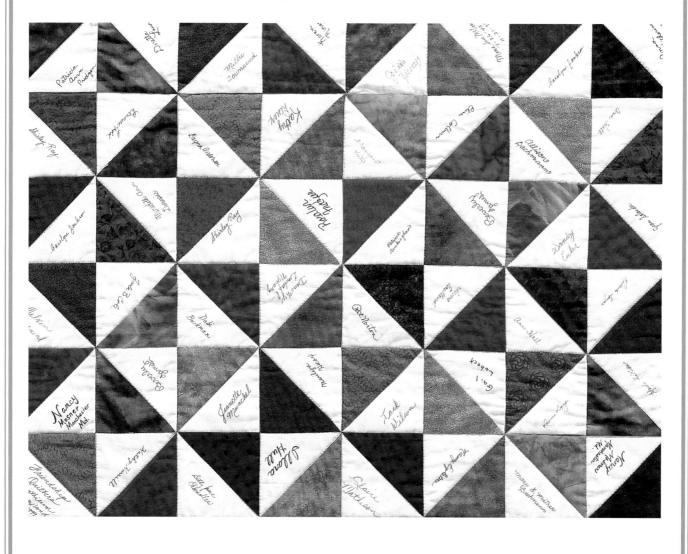

AWARENESS

What does breast-cancer awareness mean?

W E REALLY CAN'T DO anything about breast cancer just by being "aware" of it. But if we are aware, we can understand how important it is to face this problem. One out of nine women in the United States will develop breast cancer in her lifetime—a risk that was one out of fourteen in 1960. This year, a breast cancer will be newly diagnosed every three minutes, and a woman will die from breast cancer every twelve minutes. By the way, men can also get breast cancer.

Women who have regular mammograms or do monthly self-examinations are more likely to discover breast cancer in its early stages. No one wants to find out they have cancer, but early detection leads to a greater survival rate. It also means a patient may not have to be treated with chemotherapy or radiation, may not lose her hair, and may not have extensive surgery.

Breast-cancer awareness also leads to research contributions and a greater possibility for finding a cure. Pink ribbons are the symbols of breast-cancer awareness. I designed little pink-ribbon charms based on the bows in my Baltimore Bouquets patterns. My students tie them to their scissors to remind them to take care of themselves. After you read this, tie a pink ribbon to your scissors or rotary cutter, and make an appointment for your mammogram—and remind your friends to get their mammograms, too!

Paper-Pieced Ribbons

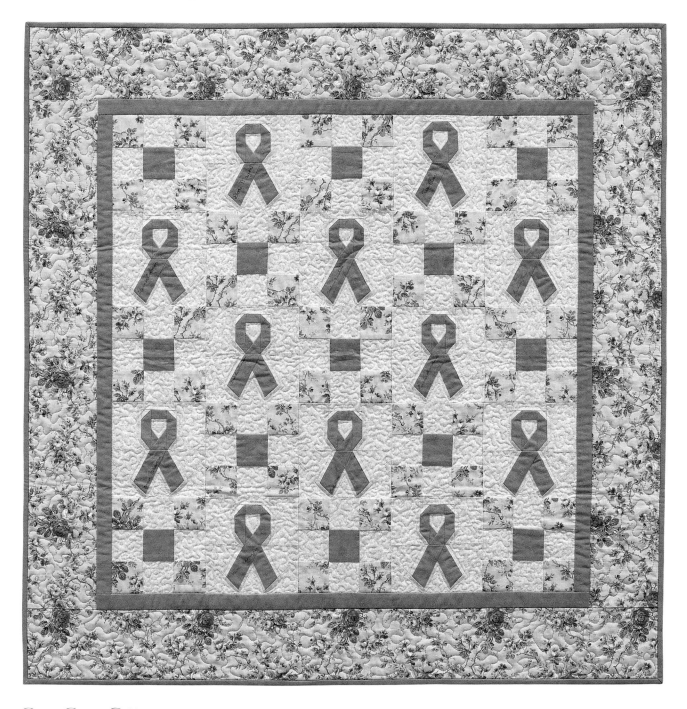

Paper-Pieced Ribbons by Mimi Dietrich, ribbon blocks designed by Carol Doak and stitched by Dori Mayer, Toni Carr, Eleanor Eckman, Barbara Jacobson, Barbara Kopf, Brenda Finnegan, Pamela Budesheim, Karan Flanscha, Chris Miller, Marian Nozinski, Dawn Schaefer, and Kay Smith, 1999, Baltimore, Maryland, 41½" x 41½"; quilted by Linda Newsom. Pink ribbons symbolizing breast-cancer awareness are easy to sew using paper-piecing techniques. Combine them with Nine Patch blocks printed with pink roses on a green background for a lovely arrangement.

Materials

(42"-wide fabric)

- 1 yd. light pink print for Paper-Pieced Ribbon blocks and Nine Patch blocks
- 1¼ yds. dark pink print for Paper-Pieced Ribbon blocks, Nine Patch blocks, inner border, and binding
- 1 yd. green print for Nine Patch blocks and outer border
- 1¼ yds. for backing
- 45" x 45" batting

Cutting

From the light pink print, cut:

- 4 strips, each 2½" x 40", for Nine Patch blocks

  Use remaining fabric for paper piecing.

From the dark pink print, cut:

- 1 strip, 2½" x 40", for Nine Patch blocks
- 2 strips, each 1½" x 30½", for inner side borders
- 2 strips, each 1½" x 32½", for inner top and bottom borders
- 5 strips, each 2" x 40", for binding

  Use remaining fabric for paper piecing.

From the green print, cut:

- 4 strips, each 2½" x 40", for Nine Patch blocks
- 2 strips, each 5" x 32½", for outer side borders
- 2 strips, each 5" x 41½", for outer top and bottom borders

Nine Patch Blocks

FINISHED SIZE: 6"

1. Sew a 2½"-wide green strip to each long edge of a 2½"-wide light pink strip. Make 2 strip sets. Use a ruler and rotary cutter to clean-cut the edges of the strip sets. Cut a total of 26 segments, each 2½" wide.

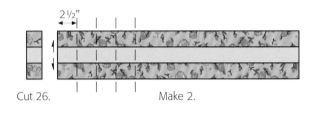

Cut 26.   Make 2.

2. Sew a 2½"-wide light pink strip to each long edge of a 2½"-wide dark pink strip. Make 1 strip set. Use a ruler and rotary cutter to clean-cut the edge of the strip set. Cut a total of 13 segments, each 2½" wide.

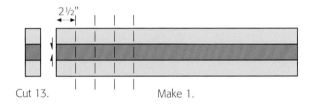

Cut 13.   Make 1.

3. Join 2 segments from step 1 and 1 segment from step 2 to complete a block.

Make 13.

Paper-Pieced Ribbon Blocks

FINISHED SIZE: 6"

TRACE THE pattern on page 15 onto light-weight paper. (Photocopying is not advised as the design may become distorted. If you must photocopy, check to make sure that each half of the design measures exactly 6½" x 3½".)

TIP: *Use a very small stitch (20 stitches per inch) and a large needle (size 90).*

---

1. Position the fabric for piece 1 over the area marked 1, right side up on the unmarked side of the paper. Hold the paper up to a light source to help you place the fabric. Pin it in place.

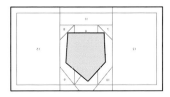

2. Place the fabric for piece 2 on top of piece 1, making sure that the fabrics extend ¼" past the line on the paper between 1 and 2. Pin the fabric in place.

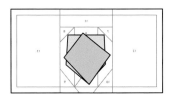

3. Place the paper block, marked side up, under your sewing machine and sew on the line between 1 and 2.

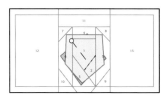

4. Trim any extra seam allowance.

5. Unfold piece 2 and press flat.

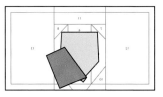

6. Continue adding pieces in numerical order until you have completed the design.

7. Use a rotary cutter and ruler to trim the edges of the block on the outer line.

8. Sew the two parts of the block together. Press this seam open.

9. Remove all paper before sewing the quilt top together.

10. Use a fine-line permanent pen to sign your name on the left streamer.

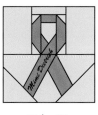

Make 12.

For more information on paper piecing, refer to Carol Doak's *Easy Machine Paper Piecing* or *Show Me How to Paper Piece,* published by That Patchwork Place.

Quilt Assembly

1. Arrange the Nine Patch blocks and Paper-Pieced Ribbon blocks as shown. Sew the blocks together to form rows. Join the rows.

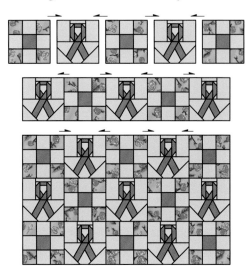

2. Sew the 1½" x 30½" inner border strips to opposite long sides of the quilt top. Sew the 1½" x 32½" inner border strips to the top and bottom edges of the quilt top.

3. Sew the 5" x 32½" outer border strips to opposite long sides of the quilt top. Sew the 5" x 41½" outer border strips to the top and bottom edges of the quilt top.

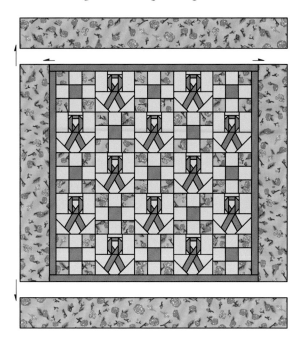

Finishing

1. Layer the quilt top with batting and backing; baste.

2. Outline-quilt around the paper-pieced ribbons. Quilt in-the-ditch on either side of the dark pink border. Free-motion quilt in the light pink area in the Nine Patch blocks and around the ribbons, and in the border.

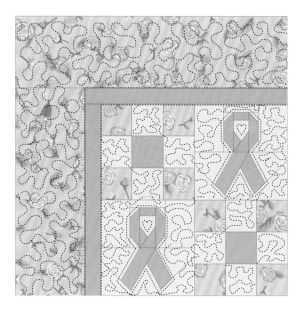

3. Bind the edges with the 2"-wide dark pink strips.

4. Add a label to the back of your quilt.

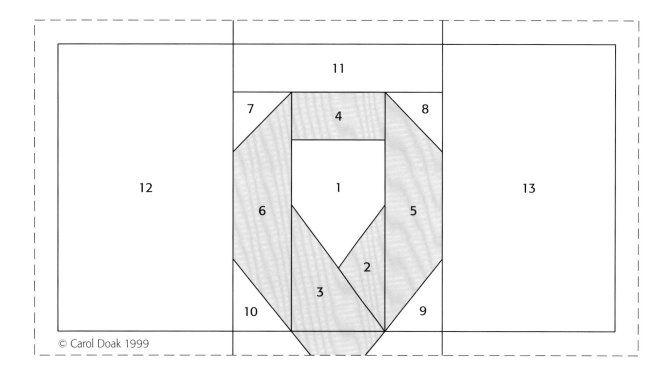

© Carol Doak 1999

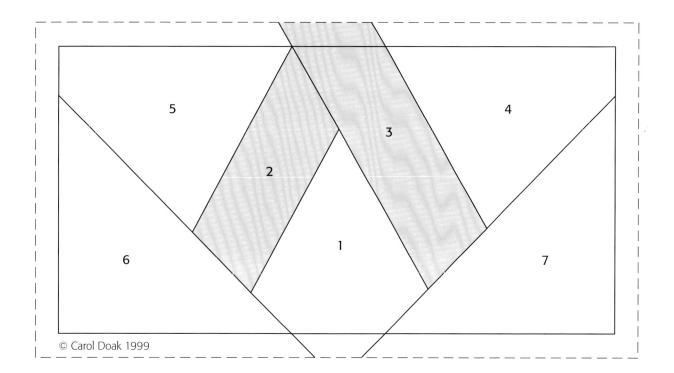

© Carol Doak 1999

POSITIVE ATTITUDES

W E ALL KNOW HOW important a positive attitude is, and that's especially true when you are ill. Quilting can really help because it gives you a goal to work toward, provides an outlet for your creativity, and takes your mind off yourself and your problem. It also allows you to choose, to be in charge of some decisions relating to colors and designs. Using delightful colors in your quilting can brighten your world.

Tips for a quilter who has breast cancer:
- *Think positive thoughts!*
- *Think about quilting.*
- *Make quilt blocks.*
- *Make quilts, but stick to little quilts so that the project is not overwhelming.*
- *Just quilt!*

If you cannot quilt because of your treatments, try doing "research." Look through magazines and books and enjoy the colors and designs. Dream about all the wonderful quilts you can make.

Sometimes quilting can be a good form of physical therapy—it gets you using your hands and arms—as long as you do not overdo things!

We all want to be in control and independent, but sometimes we need to accept help and depend on others. Maybe now it's your turn to receive help; later you will have a chance to return the favor. When a quilter in a class "lends" a scrap of fabric to another quilter, she rarely wants anything in return. I have often heard the giver say, "Please just remember this scrap and give fabric to someone later." This ribbon quilt is made with scraps of fabrics—little pieces of fabric made into a quilt.

Remember, when life gives you scraps, make a quilt!

When Life Gives You Scraps—
Make a Quilt!

When Life Gives You Scraps—Make a Quilt! by Mimi Dietrich, ribbon blocks stitched by Mary Rutter, Kathy Siuta, Eleanor Eckman, Mary Stewart, Barbara Rasch, Peggy Bonner, Marsha Vogel, Jody Schatz, Brenda Finnegan, Regina English, Lynn Irwin, Millie Tracey, Billie Meseke, Anita Askins, Jean Harmon, and MaryLou McDonald, 1999, Baltimore, Maryland, 35½" x 45½"; quilted by Linda Newsom. I love the title of this quilt! It's printed on a mug in my kitchen and always makes me smile. I used antique reproduction fabrics, although any special collection would make a great quilt.

Materials
(42"-wide fabric)

- ¼ yd. each of 9 dark prints for Scraps blocks and Appliquéd Ribbon blocks
- ¼ yd. each of 9 light prints for Scraps blocks and Appliquéd Ribbon blocks
- ⅛ yd. each of 4 dark pink prints for Appliquéd Ribbon blocks
- ⅛ yd. each of 4 light pink prints for Appliquéd Ribbon blocks
- ¼ yd. pink print for inner borders
- ⅝ yd. dark blue print for outer borders
- ⅜ yd. floral fabric for binding
- 1⅜ yds. fabric for backing
- 40" x 50" batting

Cutting

From *each* of the 9 dark prints, cut:

- 1 square, 5½" x 5½", for the Appliquéd Ribbon blocks (9 total)
- 1 square, 6¼" x 6¼", for the Scraps blocks (9 total); cut squares twice diagonally for a total of 36 triangles

From *each* of the 9 light prints, cut:

- 1 square, each 5½" x 5½", for the Appliquéd Ribbon blocks (9 total but you'll use only 8)
- 1 square, 6¼" x 6¼", for the Scraps blocks (9 total); cut squares twice diagonally for a total of 36 triangles

From the 4 dark pink prints, cut:

- 8 of ribbon template (page 20)

From the 4 light pink prints, cut:

- 9 of ribbon template (page 20)

From the pink inner border print, cut:

- 2 strips, each 1½" x 35½", for inner side borders
- 2 strips, each 1½" x 27½", for inner top and bottom borders

From the dark blue print, cut:

- 2 strips, each 4½" x 37½", for outer side borders
- 2 strips, each 4½" x 35½", for outer top and bottom borders

From the floral print, cut:

- 5 strips, each 2" x 40", for binding

Appliquéd Ribbon Blocks

FINISHED SIZE: 5"

1. Center the 5½" dark and light background squares on the full-size appliqué pattern on page 20 and trace the design.

2. Using your favorite technique, appliqué light ribbons on dark backgrounds and dark ribbons on light backgrounds.

3. Use a fine-line permanent pen to draw 2 lines to define the ribbon streamer. Write your name on the right-hand streamer.

Make 17.

Scraps Blocks

FINISHED SIZE: 5"

JOIN 2 DARK triangles and 2 light triangles as shown to make a block. Be sure to use 4 different prints for each block.

Make 18.

Quilt Assembly

1. Arrange the Appliquéd Ribbon blocks and Scraps blocks as shown, placing blocks with dark prints next to light prints to create the star design. Sew the blocks together to form rows. Join the rows.

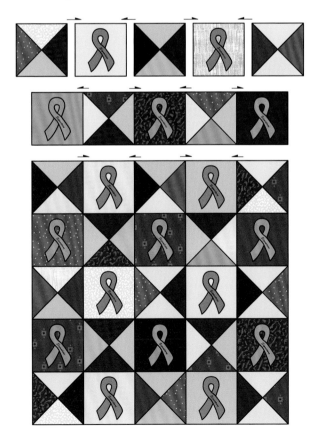

2. Sew the 1½" x 35½" inner border strips to opposite long sides of the quilt top. Sew the 1½" x 27½" inner border strips to the top and bottom edges of the quilt top.

3. Sew the 4½" x 37½" outer border strips to opposite long sides of the quilt top. Sew the 4½" x 35½" outer border strips to the top and bottom edges of the quilt top.

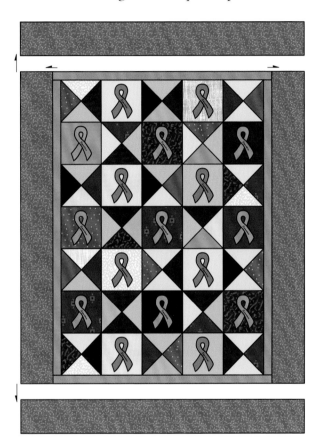

Finishing

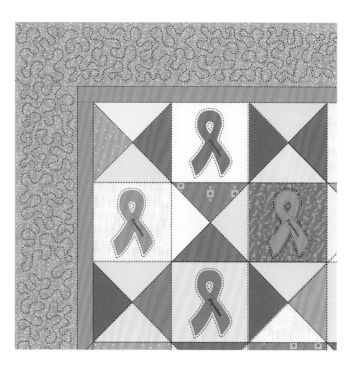

1. Layer the quilt top with batting and backing; baste.

2. Outline-quilt around the pink ribbons. Quilt in-the-ditch around the patchwork pieces and on either side of the inner borders. Free-motion quilt in the outer border.

3. Bind the edges with the 2"-wide floral print strips.

4. Add a label to the back of your quilt.

Draw lines with permanent pen when appliqué is complete.

Signature

TIPS

Here are a few hints for making blocks or a quilt for a quilter who has breast cancer.

+ Use your friend's favorite fabrics and colors.

+ Make easy blocks you can complete in a short time. Mail them one at a time to give her a surprise in the mail each day.

+ Give her the blocks to put together but include a kit with batting, backing, and binding.

+ Sew the blocks together and give her a quilt top. When she feels well enough, she will love reading the names of friends as she quilts the top. When you make a quilt for a quilter who has breast cancer, be aware of how sick she is. If her quilting arm is involved, or if she is receiving chemotherapy, she may not be able to quilt it herself. On the other hand, quilting may provide good physical and mental therapy.

+ Machine quilt the top and give it to her, ready to enjoy.

FAMILY

*I*F SOMEONE IS DIAGNOSED with breast cancer, it is not just the patient that is affected by the disease. Cancer impacts the entire family. Just like the pattern of woven ribbons in this quilt and pillow, the patterns of our lives as a family are woven tightly together. Everyday routines and schedules are changed by visits to the doctor or treatments. Family members are worried and may be frustrated by added responsibilities. Relatives may feel helpless at such a time and would love to participate in an easy quilting project, feeling that they are doing something positive. Family members will be grateful that you asked them to be a part of such a special gift.

- *Use easy strip-quilting methods to make the blocks for the Woven Ribbon quilt.*
- *Use the patient's favorite colors for the Woven Ribbons.*
- *Send the blocks to family members.*
- *Write a note inviting them to sign the block with their name or a message.*
- *Have them mail the block back to you, or to the patient.*
- *Give them a deadline within a few days and include a self-addressed stamped envelope.*
- *Hang the blocks on a clothesline in the patient's room before you sew them together into a quilt.*

Here are some suggestions for messages:

- *To my favorite sister (especially if she's your only sister)*
- *When this you see, remember me!*
- *You are loved!*
- *This too shall pass*
- *Follow the Yellow Brick Road*

- *I'm only a phone call away*
- *You are always in my heart (draw a little heart)*
- *I was thinking about you today (draw a happy face)*
- *The sun will come out tomorrow (draw a sun)*
- *Rain helps the flowers grow (draw a flower)*
- *XOXOXO*

Woven Ribbons

Woven Ribbons by Mimi Dietrich, 1999, Baltimore, Maryland, 34¼" x 41¾"; quilted by Linda Newsom. This quilt can be personalized by using someone's two favorite colors. The white strips are quilted with pink and purple thread; they can also be signed by family or friends.

Materials

(42"-wide fabric)

- ½ yd. pink print for Rail Fence blocks
- ½ yd. purple print for Rail Fence blocks
- ½ yd. white-on-white print for Rail Fence blocks
- 1 yd. pink-and-purple print for borders and binding
- 1⅜ yds. for backing
- 38" x 46" batting

Cutting

From the pink print, cut:

- 8 strips, each 1¾" x 40", for Rail Fence blocks

From the purple print, cut:

- 8 strips, each 1¾" x 40", for Rail Fence blocks

From the white-on-white print, cut:

- 8 strips, each 1¾" x 40", for Rail Fence blocks

From the pink-and-purple print, cut:

- 4 strips, each 4¼" x 34¼", for borders
- 5 strips, each 2" x 40", for binding

Block Assembly

FINISHED SIZE: 3¾"

1. Sew a 1¾"-wide pink strip to each long edge of a 1¾"-wide white strip. Make 4 strip sets. Use a ruler and rotary cutter to clean-cut the edges of the strip sets. Cut a total of 32 segments, each 4¼" wide.

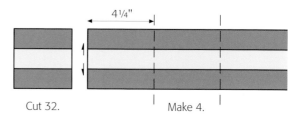

Cut 32.   Make 4.

2. Sew a 1¾"-wide purple strip to each long edge of a 1¾"-wide white strip. Make 4 strip sets. Use a ruler and rotary cutter to clean-cut the edges of the strip sets. Cut a total of 31 segments, each 4¼" wide.

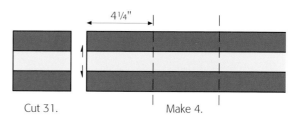

Cut 31.   Make 4.

3. Use a fine-line permanent pen to sign your name or write a message in the center of each block.

Quilt Assembly

1. Arrange the pink-and-purple Rail Fence blocks as shown. Sew the blocks together to form rows. Join the rows.

2. Sew 4¼" x 34¼" border strips to opposite long sides of the quilt top. Sew 4¼" x 34¼" border strips to the top and bottom edges of the quilt top.

Finishing

1. Layer the quilt top with batting and backing; baste.

2. Quilt in-the-ditch around the squares. Free-motion quilt in the border. If desired, do additional quilting in the white-on-white areas.

3. Bind the edges with the 2"-wide pink-and-purple strips.

4. Add a label to the back of your quilt.

Woven Ribbons Pillow

Woven Ribbons Pillow by Norma Campbell, 1999, Arnold, Maryland, 12" x 12". A pillow is a welcome gift for a patient who has had surgery. She can rest her arm on the soft pillow to keep it elevated and away from her incision. A pillow with notes of encouragement will bring warm wishes. It's also a great conversation starter!

Materials
(42"-wide fabric)

- ⅛ yd. pink print for Rail Fence blocks
- ⅛ yd. purple print for Rail Fence blocks
- ⅛ yd. white-on-white print for Rail Fence blocks
- ⅜ yd. pink-and-purple print for backing
- 12" pillow form

Cutting

From the pink print, cut:
- 2 strips, each 1½" x 40", for Rail Fence blocks

From the purple print, cut:
- 2 strips, each 1½" x 40", for Rail Fence blocks

From the white-on-white print, cut:
- 2 strips, each 1½" x 40", for Rail Fence blocks

From the pink-and-purple print, cut:
- 1 square, 12½" x 12½", for backing

Block Assembly
FINISHED SIZE: 3"

1. Sew a 1½"-wide pink strip to each long edge of a 1½"-wide white strip. Use a ruler and rotary cutter to clean-cut the edges of the strip sets. Cut a total of 8 blocks, each 3½" wide.

Cut 8.   Make 1.

2. Sew a 1½"-wide purple strip to each long edge of a 1½"-wide white strip. Use a ruler and rotary cutter to clean-cut the edges of the strip sets. Cut a total of 8 blocks, each 3½" wide.

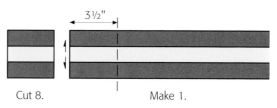

Cut 8.   Make 1.

3. Use a fine-line permanent pen to sign your name or write a message in the center of each block.

Pillow Assembly

1. Arrange the pink and purple Rail Fence blocks as shown. Sew the blocks together to form rows. Join the rows.

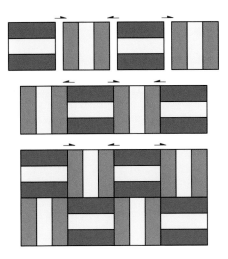

2. Place the pillow top right sides together with the backing. Pin, then sew around the edges, leaving an opening on one side.

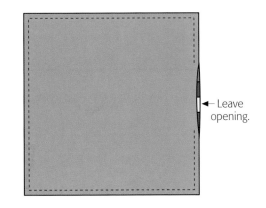

←Leave opening.

3. Turn the pillow right side out.

4. Insert the pillow form.

5. Hand stitch the side opening closed.

GRANDMOTHERS, MOTHERS, DAUGHTERS, AND SISTERS

RANDMOTHERS, MOTHERS, daughters, and sisters (does that include all of us!) are probably most concerned about breast cancer because we worry about a genetic link between us. These women are our closest support group. A breast cancer in the family is a time to help each other and share responsibilities.

Women are very good at nurturing and understanding each other. Think what you would need in a time like this. Just a small gift of time, such as having lunch together, sharing a book or magazine, or stitching together, can mean a lot.

A patient who spent three weeks in the hospital writes, "My oldest daughter spent several nights with me. It was lovely to see her sweet face when I awoke." Her youngest daughter lives far away, but she kept in touch by phone almost every day. "She researched my cancer. It was good for us to be able to talk about my cancer together."

Six quilters made the Buttons and Bows quilt. We are connected to twelve grandmothers, six mothers, five daughters, and thirteen sisters. We made these pink blocks for them.

Now is the time to tell the women in your life that you love them and care about them. Put a pink button in your pocket or tie a pink ribbon around your finger to remind yourself to do something special for one of them today.

Buttons and Bows

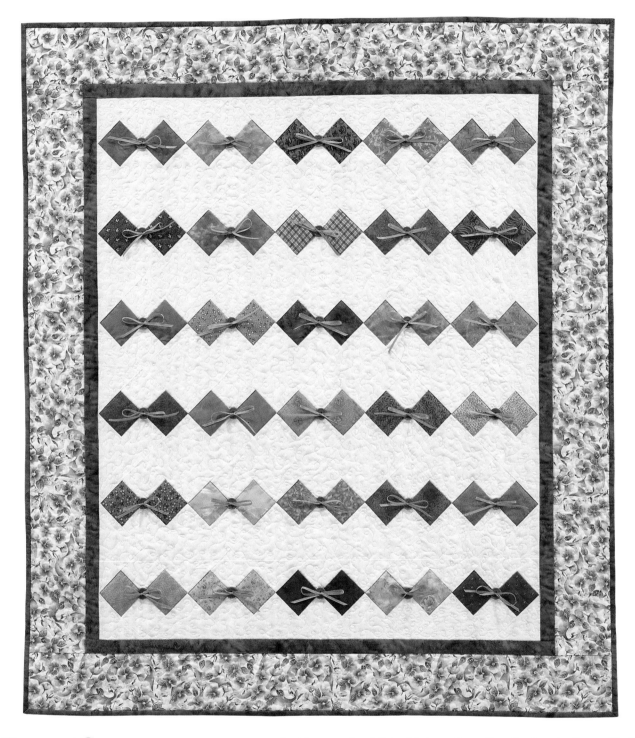

Buttons and Bows by Mimi Dietrich, blocks stitched by Monday Night Madness, Joan Costello, Laurie Gregg, Phyllis Hess, Barbara McMahon, Vivian Schafer, 1999, Baltimore, Maryland, 37" x 42½"; quilted by Linda Newsom. These easy Four Patch blocks are fun to make with a collection of pink fabrics. The buttons and ribbons add a three-dimensional touch.

Materials

(42"-wide fabric)

- 30 different pink print rectangles, each 2½" x 5"
- 1⅛ yds. white-on-white print for Four Patch blocks, setting squares, and side setting triangles
- ⅝ yd. pink solid for inner borders and binding
- ½ yd. dark pink print for outer borders
- 1⅜ yds. for backing
- 30 pink buttons
- 10 yds. ¼"-wide pink ribbon
- 41" x 46" batting

Cutting

From *each* pink print rectangle, cut:
- 2 squares, each 2½" x 2½", for Four Patch blocks (60 total)

From the white-on-white print, cut:
- 4 strips, each 2½" x 40"; crosscut strips into a total of 60 squares, each 2½" x 2½", for Four Patch blocks
- 3 strips, each 4½" x 40"; crosscut strips into a total of 20 squares, each 4½" x 4½", for setting squares
- 1 strip, 6⅞" x 40"; crosscut strip into 5 squares, each 6⅞" x 6⅞"; cut squares twice diagonally for a total of 20 side setting triangles (you will have 2 extra triangles)
- 2 squares, each 3¾" x 3¾"; cut squares once diagonally for a total of 4 corner setting triangles

From the pink solid, cut:
- 2 strips, each 1½" x 34½", for inner side borders
- 2 strips, each 1½" x 31", for inner top and bottom borders
- 5 strips, each 2" x 40", for binding

From the dark pink print, cut:
- 2 strips, each 3½" x 36½", for outer side borders
- 2 strips, each 3½" x 37", for outer top and bottom borders

Block Assembly

FINISHED SIZE: 4"

JOIN 2 WHITE and 2 matching pink squares as shown to make a Four Patch block.

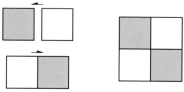

Make 30.

Quilt Assembly

1. Arrange the Four Patch blocks, setting squares, and side setting triangles as shown. Sew the blocks and triangles together to form diagonal rows.

2. Join the rows, adding the corner setting triangles last.

3. Sew the 1½" x 34½" inner border strips to
   opposite long sides of the quilt top. Sew the
   1½" x 31" inner border strips to the top and
   bottom edges of the quilt top.

4. Sew the 3½" x 36½" outer border strips to
   opposite long sides of the quilt top. Sew the
   3½" x 37" outer border strips to the top and
   bottom edges of the quilt top.

Finishing

1. Layer the quilt top with batting and backing; baste.

2. Quilt in-the-ditch around the bows and on
   either side of the pink border. Free-motion
   quilt in the white squares and triangles, and
   in the border.

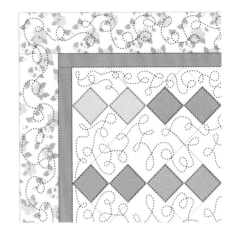

3. Bind the edges with the 2"-wide pink solid
   strips.

4. Cut the ¼"-wide ribbon into 30 pieces,
   each 12" long. Fold each piece of ribbon in
   half and stitch it to the center of each Four
   Patch block. Thread the ribbon through the
   holes in a button and tie a bow to hold the
   button on the quilt.

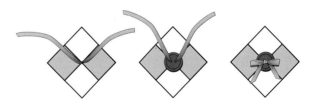

TIP: *Add a dab of clear nail polish in the
center of each bow to keep it secure.*

5. Add a label to the back of your quilt.

FRIENDS

A FRIEND TOLD ME it was so hard to go visit a friend with cancer, but it was important to go see her—for both of them.

Tips for a quilter whose friend has breast cancer:

+ *Call; start your conversation by saying "Hi, I'm thinking of you today!" Try not to ask "How are you?"*
+ *Visit (bring chocolate).*
+ *Send funny cards (it's great to laugh).*
+ *Send touching cards (it's okay to cry).*
+ *Send fat quarters of fabric (but only pretty colors).*
+ *Send quilt blocks (to be made into a quilt later).*
+ *Make her a quilt.*
+ *Make her a meal.*
+ *Let her know that she is in your prayers—she will feel strength from your thoughts.*
+ *Try not to be afraid for your friend—she's already afraid and that's enough. Be strong in her presence.*
+ *Try to take her mind off her condition, but let her talk if she needs to. Sometimes just listening can be the best thing.*
+ *Volunteer to take her to the doctor or to a treatment.*
+ *Be there for her.*
+ *Be her friend.*

Friendship Ribbons

Friendship Ribbons by Mimi Dietrich, ribbon blocks stitched by Penny Clifton and Libbie Rollman, 1999, Baltimore, Maryland, 35½" x 35½"; quilted by Linda Newsom. Strategic placement of the bright pink fabric accents the ribbons in this version of the traditional Friendship Star block design.

Materials

(42"-wide fabric)

- ¾ yd. pink print for Friendship Star blocks and inner border
- ⅞ yd. light teal print for Friendship Star blocks and outer border
- ½ yd. dark teal print for Friendship Star blocks and binding
- 1⅛ yds. fabric for backing
- 40" x 40" batting

Cutting

From the pink print, cut:

- 2 strips, each 1½" x 27½", for inner side borders
- 2 strips, each 1½" x 29½", for inner top and bottom borders
- 4 strips, each 3⅞" x 40"; crosscut strips into a total of 36 squares, each 3⅞" x 3⅞"; cut squares once diagonally for a total of 72 triangles for Friendship Star blocks

From the light teal print, cut:

- 2 strips, each 3½" x 29½", for outer side borders
- 2 strips, each 3½" x 35½", for outer top and bottom borders
- 1 strip, 3½" x 40"; crosscut strip into 9 squares, each 3½" x 3½", for Friendship Star blocks
- 2 strips, each 3⅞" x 40"; crosscut strips into a total of 18 squares, each 3⅞" x 3⅞"; cut squares once diagonally for a total of 36 triangles for Friendship Star blocks

From the dark teal print, cut:

- 4 strips, each 2" x 40", for binding
- 2 strips, each 3⅞" x 40"; crosscut strips into a total of 18 squares, each 3⅞" x 3⅞"; cut squares once diagonally for a total of 36 triangles for Friendship Star blocks

Block Assembly

FINISHED SIZE: 9"

1. Join a light teal triangle and a pink triangle.

Make 36.

2. Join a dark teal triangle and a pink triangle.

Make 36.

3. Arrange the triangle units as shown, with a light teal square in the center. Sew the units together to form rows. Join the rows.

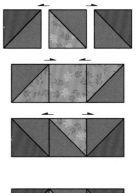

Make 9.

Quilt Assembly

1. Arrange the Friendship Star blocks as shown. Sew the squares together to form rows. Join the rows.

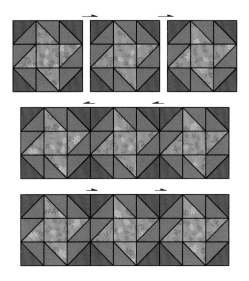

2. Sew the 1½" x 27½" inner border strips to opposite sides of the quilt top. Sew the 1½" x 29½" inner border strips to the top and bottom edges of the quilt top.

3. Sew the 3½" x 29½" outer border strips to opposite sides of the quilt top. Sew the 3½" x 35½" outer border strips to the top and bottom edges of the quilt top.

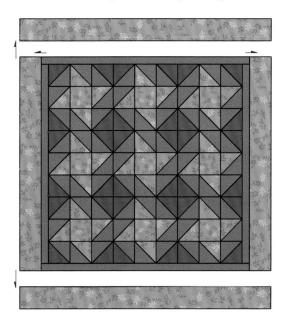

Finishing

1. Layer the quilt top with batting and backing; baste.

2. Quilt in-the-ditch around the pink "ribbons" and on either side of the pink border. Free-motion quilt using different colors in the stars, ribbons, and dark teal squares. Free-motion quilt in the border.

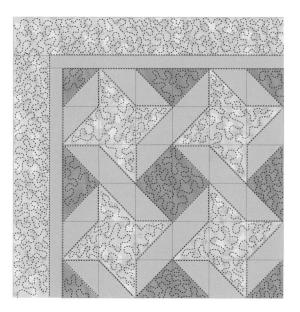

3. Bind the edges with the 2"-wide dark teal strips.

4. Add a label to the back of your quilt.

CAREGIVERS

*M*ANY DOCTORS FEEL THAT surrounding patients with good feelings and caring can make a real clinical difference in their recovery. Patients can actually feel a strength and peace that comes from the positive thoughts of family and friends.

Who is a caregiver?

- *A friend who calls, visits, or e-mails!*
- *A friend who keeps in touch*
- *A friend who listens*
- *A friend who shares a laugh*
- *A friend who shares a cry*
- *A friend who shares a hug*
- *A friend who goes to a doctor's appointment*
- *A friend who brings lunch to share*
- *A friend who brings chocolate*
- *A friend who cooks a meal to help the primary caregiver*
- *A friend who brings her doll to visit*
- *A friend who buys an extra large T-shirt*
- *A friend who makes a quilt block*
- *A dear friend who just "cares"*

If you have been the recipient of special "care," make this little quilt and tie it to a little hanger to thank your caregiver.

Thank You Dear Friend

Thank You Dear Friend by Mimi Dietrich, 1999, Baltimore, Maryland, 6½" x 6½". Little things mean a lot, and this little quilt can be made to show someone how much you appreciate their support. This quilt is hand appliquéd, but the design could also be fused or machine appliquéd.

Materials

(42"-wide fabric)

- ¼ yd. off-white print for appliqué background square and backing
- 5" square of light blue print for appliquéd pot
- 5" square of dark blue print for appliquéd pot rim
- 5" square of green print for appliquéd leaves
- ⅛ yd. pink print for appliquéd heart and binding
- 8" x 8" batting
- ½ yd. ¼"-wide pink ribbon

Cutting

From the off-white print, cut:

- 2 squares, each 6½" x 6½", for background square and backing

From the light blue print, cut:

- 1 of template 1

From the dark blue print, cut:

- 1 of template 2

From the green print, cut:

- 2 of template 4, placing the leaves on the bias

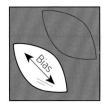

From the pink print, cut:

- 1 strip, 2" x 36", for binding
- 1 of template 3, placing the heart shape on the bias

Block Assembly

FINISHED SIZE: 6"

1. Center the 6½" background square on the full size appliqué pattern (page 40) and trace the appliqué design.

2. Iron a 6" square of freezer paper on the wrong side of the background square to stabilize the fabric. Trace the words from the pattern onto the background fabric using a fine-line permanent marker. Remove the freezer paper.

3. Appliqué the pot; position the top of the pot above the line for the pot rim.

4. Appliqué the pot rim, covering the top edge of the pot.

5. Appliqué the heart and leaves.

Finishing

1. Layer the quilt top with batting and backing; baste.

2. Quilt in-the-ditch around the appliqué pieces.

3. Bind the edges with the 2"-wide pink strips.

4. Add a label to the back of your quilt.

5. To display your quilt, tie your quilt to a doll's dress hanger with pink ribbon (see "Resources" on page 80).

Thank You Dear Friend

3

4

4

2

1

Little Heart

SMALL QUILTS

FINISHED SIZE: 5¾" x 5¾"

YOU CAN ALSO use just one block to make a small quilt. Write a special message on the block, then layer it with batting and backing, bind it, and quilt it. Tie the finished miniquilt to a small hanger with pink bows.

Let a friend know she's loved with a darling little quilt. All the quilts shown in the photo are based on block designs found elsewhere in this book, with the exception of the Little Heart quilt. If that's the design you want to make, use the following directions and the Little Heart template at left. The fabrics shown are from the "Quilt for a Cure" collection.

- ✦ 4½" square of rose fabric for the appliqued heart
- ✦ 4½" square of off-white fabric for the background

- ✦ 2 squares, each 3¾" x 3¾", of pink fabric for the corner triangles. Cut squares once diagonally.
- ✦ 6½" square for backing
- ✦ 6½" square of batting
- ✦ 2" x 40" strip for binding
- ✦ ½ yd. ¼"-wide deep rose ribbon

1. Appliqué a heart on the background square as shown.

2. Sew the pink triangles to the corners of the background square.

3. Finish as directed on page 37.

HEALTH-CARE PROFESSIONALS

*M*ARY RUTTER IS AN oncology nurse who is also a quilter. She feels honored to be a nurse, and comes to quilt class with wonderful stories that warm our hearts. Mary tells us that she meets heroes every day—cancer patients who face treatments with strength, courage, and even humor. One of her most memorable patients wore a T-shirt and shorts and brought a beach ball to her radiation treatment to ease her fears. She imagined that she was relaxing on a beach—what a positive attitude!

Mary sees how much a heartfelt gift from a relative or friend means to a hospital patient. When a quilt is placed on a bed, one can literally cover themselves in the good wishes of others. A wall quilt brightens the hospital room because a quilt is a "work of heart."

I have met doctors, nurses, technicians, receptionists, and office personnel who treated me with respect, care, and a positive attitude. I love doctors who provide hugs of strength with bad news and hugs of happiness with good news.

I love the humor, too. Health-care professionals meet scared people every day and they can help us relax and feel comfortable. The surgeon's receptionist who asked me if I was there for "the girls," just to confirm I was there for breast surgery, made me smile.

The most powerful thing a doctor ever said to me was "Just because you have cancer does not mean you have to die." I think about that sentence a lot. It's true.

This quilt was made in heartfelt appreciation for our health-care professionals who provide strength and compassion as they encounter cancer patients every day.

Heartfelt Appreciation

Heartfelt Appreciation by Mimi Dietrich, arranged by the staff at Seminole Sampler, 1999, Baltimore, Maryland, 28" x 28"; quilted by Linda Newsom. A new product is the secret to stitching these little squares together. Dark and light floral print squares are fused to a lightweight interfacing to keep them in place for stitching. This design produces a special quilt made "from the heart." Floral fabrics used in the quilt are from the Garden Twist Collection from In The Beginning Fabrics.

Materials
(42"-wide fabric)

- ⅔ yd. floral with dark background for heart squares and outer borders
- ½ yd. floral with light background for background squares
- ½ yd. pink print for inner borders and binding
- 1 yd. for backing
- 32" x 32" batting
- ¾ yd. Quilt-Fuse or lightweight fusible interfacing

Cutting

From the floral with dark background, cut:

- 2 strips, each 3½" x 22", for outer side borders
- 2 strips, each 3½" x 28", for outer top and bottom borders
- 3 strips, each 2" x 40"; crosscut strips into a total of 60 squares, each 2" x 2"★

From the floral with light background, cut:

- 7 strips, each 2" x 40"; crosscut strips into a total of 140 squares, each 2" x 2"★

From the pink print, cut:

- 2 strips, each 1½" x 20", for inner side borders
- 2 strips, each 1½" x 22", for inner top and bottom borders
- 4 strips, each 2" x 40", for binding

★*This includes extra squares so you'll have plenty to choose from when arranging your heart.*

Quilt Top Assembly

			O	O						O	O			
		O	X	X	O				O	X	X	O		
	O	X	X	X	X	O	X	X	X	X	O			
O	X	X	O	O	X	X	X	O	O	X	X	O		
O	X	X	O		O	X	O		O	X	X	O		
O	X	X	O			O			O	X	X	O		
O	X	X	O						O	X	X	O		
	O	X	X	O				O	X	X	O			
		O	X	X	O		O	X	X	O				
			O	X	X	O	X	X	O					
				O	X	X	X	O						
					O	X	O							
						O								

 X — Dark floral squares

O — Light floral squares with partial leaves and flowers

☐ — Light floral squares with least amount of flowers and leaves

ASSEMBLING AND SEWING this block is very easy using a new product called Quilt-Fuse, a lightweight fusible interfacing marked with a 2"-square grid. If you cannot find Quilt-Fuse, use a #2 pencil to mark a 2" grid on lightweight fusible interfacing.

1. Cut a 26" x 26" square of marked interfacing and place it on a flat surface with the fusible side up. If possible, tape it to a wall so that you can stand and view the arrangement at a distance.

2. Referring to the diagram, place squares cut from the floral with dark background on each square marked with an X. Use squares that are densely printed with flowers and leaves.

3. To soften the heart edges, use squares cut from the floral with light background that have flowers and leaves printed on only part of them. Look for partially printed fabric squares for the cleavage, the point, and the sides of the heart. Referring to the diagram

on page 44, carefully arrange these in the squares marked with an O.

4. Use floral with light background squares that contain fewer flowers and leaves to fill in the remaining blank squares.

5. Iron the squares to the interfacing, following the manufacturer's directions.

6. Working in the vertical direction, fold each row of squares over the adjoining row, right sides together, and sew a ¼" seam. Stitch all the vertical rows in this manner.

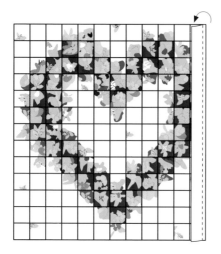

   Carefully cut the fold of the seam allowances and press them open to reduce bulk.

7. Working in the horizontal direction, fold each row of squares over the adjoining row and sew a ¼" seam. Stitch all the horizontal rows in this manner. Carefully cut the fold of the seam allowances and press them open.

8. Sew the 1½" x 20" inner border strips to opposite sides of the quilt top. Sew the 1½" x 22" inner border strips to the top and bottom edges of the quilt top.

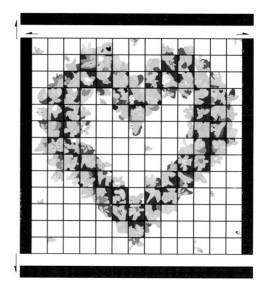

9. Sew the 3½" x 22" outer border strips to opposite sides of the quilt top. Sew the 3½" x 28" outer border strips to the top and bottom edges of the quilt top.

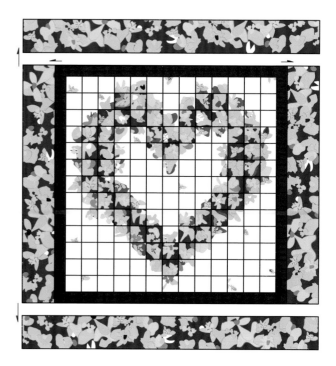

Finishing

1. Layer the quilt top with batting and back-ing; baste.

2. Quilt in-the-ditch on either side of the pink border. Free-motion quilt lines around the heart and in the border.

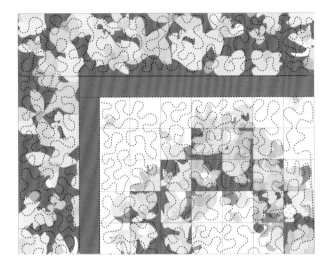

3. Bind the edges with the 2"-wide pink strips.

4. Add a label to the back of your quilt.

SURVIVORS AND SUPPORT GROUPS

*T*HINK OF ALL CANCER patients as survivors, not victims. It has taken me almost five years just to be able to say the word "survivor." An everyday reminder of breast cancer is a little twinge in your arm on the side of your surgery. When surgeons do a lumpectomy or mastectomy, they remove lymph nodes to test them for the spread of cancer. Sometimes this results in a condition called lymphedema, a swelling in the arm, because the lymph nodes are no longer there to help move fluid through your system. This affects quilters because too much lifting (heavy quilts), pressure (pushing a needle through thick batting), or injury (sticking with needles) can affect the swelling. Quilters may need to change their style of quilting to help this condition. Make small quilts instead of large ones. Use lighter batting for hand quilting. Try machine piecing or machine appliqué instead of handwork. The quilting world has many wonderful methods for accomplishing the art of quilting, allowing us to express our creativity and have fun with wonderful fabrics.

Can a support group of quilters/survivors be fun? Of course. We have five quilters in our support group and we have lunches together, walk together in the Race for the Cure (and then go out to brunch), and sew together. When one person's arm is tired from rotary cutting or machine sewing, we just switch jobs. One day at lunch we discovered that two members had the same nickname for their breast prosthesis—Gertrude! That was a day for friendship and laughter, and it gave us a name for our group—the Gertrudes!

We share the knowledge that there are more important things in life than perfectly matched patchwork points. Breast cancer has changed our lives.

Rosebuds for Recovery

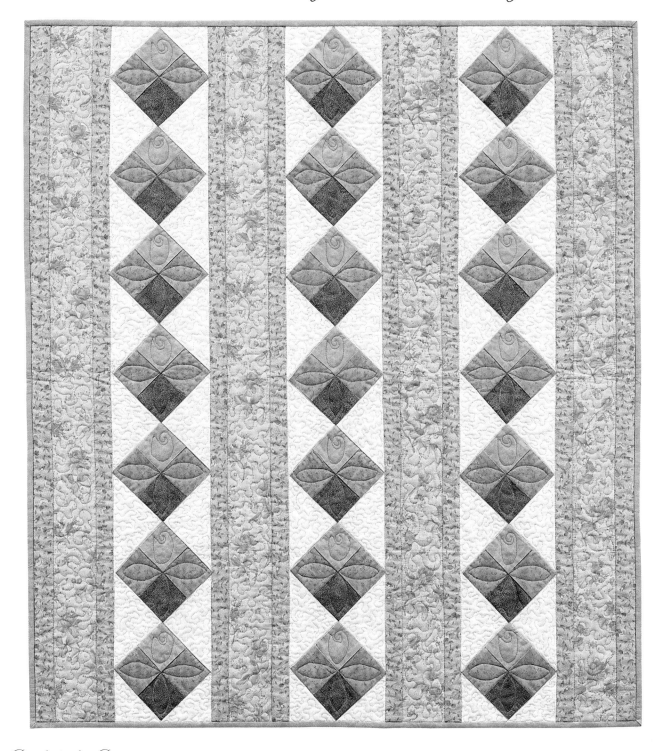

Rosebuds for Recovery by Mimi Dietrich, stitched by Siobhan Breen, Sue Brunt, Mimi Dietrich, Patti Muller, Helen Quane, 1999, Baltimore, Maryland, 35½" x 40⅛"; quilted by Linda Newsom. Easy Four Patch blocks become rosebuds with pink and green fabrics. This strippy-style quilt is a creative arrangement for blocks and borders.

- ½ yd. pink print for Four Patch blocks and binding
- ⅜ yd. light green print for Four Patch blocks
- ¼ yd. dark green print for Four Patch blocks
- ½ yd. blue print for accent strips
- ½ yd. floral print for wide strips
- ⅝ yd. cream print for setting triangles
- 1¼ yds. for backing
- 40" x 44" batting

Cutting

From the pink print, cut:

- 2 strips, each 2½" x 40"; crosscut strips into a total of 21 squares, each 2½" x 2½", for Four Patch blocks
- 4 strips, each 2" x 40", for binding

From the light green print, cut:

- 3 strips, each 2½" x 40"; crosscut strips into a total of 42 squares, each 2½" x 2½", for Four Patch blocks

From the dark green print, cut:

- 2 strips, each 2½" x 40"; crosscut strips into a total of 21 squares, each 2½" x 2½", for Four Patch blocks

From the blue print, cut:

- 8 strips, each 1½" x 40⅛", for accent strips

From the floral print, cut:

- 4 strips, each 3" x 40⅛", for wide strips

From the cream print, cut:

- 2 strips, each 6⅞" x 40"; crosscut strips into a total of 9 squares, each 6⅞" x 6⅞"; cut squares twice diagonally for a total of 36 side setting triangles
- 1 strip, 3¾" x 40"; crosscut strip into 6 squares, each 3¾" x 3¾"; cut squares once diagonally for a total of 12 corner setting triangles

Block Assembly

FINISHED SIZE: 4"

JOIN 1 PINK, 1 dark green, and 2 light green squares as shown to make a Four Patch block.

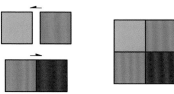

Make 21.

Quilt Assembly

1. Arrange the Four Patch blocks and side setting triangles as shown. Sew the blocks and triangles together in diagonal rows.

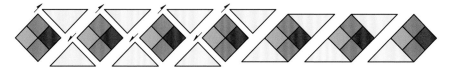

2. Join the rows, adding the corner setting tri-angles last. Make 3 strips of Four Patch blocks.

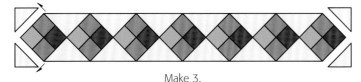

Make 3.

3. Sew a 1½" x 40⅛" blue print accent strip to each long edge of a 3" x 40⅛" long floral print strip. Make 4 strips.

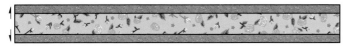

Make 4.

4. Arrange the floral strips and Four Patch strips as shown. Sew the strips together to complete the quilt top.

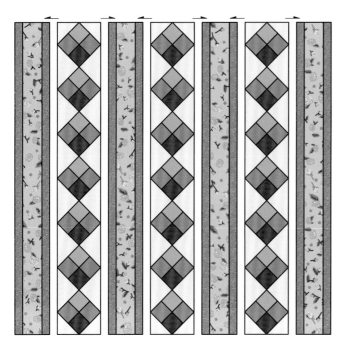

Finishing

1. Layer the quilt top with batting and backing; baste.

2. Quilt in-the-ditch on either side of the blue accent strips and around the Four Patch blocks. Free-motion quilt in the floral strips. Quilt leaves and rosebuds in the Four Patch blocks.

3. Bind the edges with the 2"-wide pink strips.

4. Add a label to the back of your quilt.

GROUP QUILTS

*W*HEN THINGS GO WRONG, wouldn't we all like to throw dishes against a brick wall? Quilters can help by piecing these blocks together! The pattern in this quilt, Broken Dishes, is made up of four small units that are easy to make as a group quilt.

A group quilt needs a leader to organize making the quilt. Here are some hints:

- *Keep notes about the quilt and a list of people participating in the project.*
- *Plan easy blocks for the group to make.*
- *Show the group a drawing or photo of the proposed quilt.*
- *Sew a sample block to show to the group.*
- *Give each person a "kit" in a small plastic bag, including a drawing of the block, clear directions, and ample fabric in case of mistakes.*
- *Include a phone number in case they need help.*
- *Include a self-addressed envelope to return the block to the organizer.*
- *Set a reasonable deadline and allow a few days for late stitchers.*
- *Organize a small committee to complete the quilt top.*
- *Set the deadline to allow time for the committee to complete the top.*

The size of your quilt may depend on the number of blocks you receive. You may want to complete the center of the quilt before choosing the border fabrics. This quilt can be made any size and will look colorful and cheerful if you use jewel-tone prints.

Broken Dishes

Broken Dishes by Mimi Dietrich, blocks stitched by The Friendship Quilters, 1999, Linthicum, Maryland, 37½" x 44½"; quilted by Linda Newsom. This group quilt was made from jewel-tone fabrics that make the Broken Dishes blocks sparkle!

Materials

(42"-wide fabric)

- ⅞ yd. off-white solid for patchwork triangles
- ⅞ yd. *total* assorted jewel-tone prints for patchwork triangles
- ¼ yd. purple print for inner border
- ⅞ yd. pink print for outer border and binding
- 1⅜ yds. for backing
- 42" x 49" batting
- Metallic thread for quilting

Cutting

From the off-white solid, cut:

- 5 strips, each 5" x 40"; crosscut strips into a total of 40 squares, each 5" x 5", for Broken Dishes blocks

From the assorted jewel-tone prints, cut:

- 40 squares, each 5" x 5", for Broken Dishes blocks

From the purple print, cut:

- 2 strips, each 1½" x 35½", for inner side borders
- 2 strips, each 1½" x 30½", for inner top and bottom borders

From the pink print, cut:

- 4 strips, each 4" x 37½", for outer borders
- 5 strips, each 2" x 40", for binding

Block Assembly

FINISHED SIZE: 7"

1. Place an off-white square on top of a jewel-tone square, right sides together. Use a pencil and ruler to draw a diagonal line on the off-white square. Draw a line ¼" on either side of the center line.

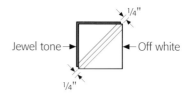

2. Sew on the ¼" lines. Cut on the marked center diagonal line. Press the seams toward the dark fabrics. You have just made 2 pieced units!

3. Trim the pieced squares to 4" x 4". You can use a 4" square ruler to trim the squares.

4. Sign your name or write a personal message on the off-white side of the square with a fine-line permanent pen. Place the square on top of the full-size drawing on facing page and try to keep your name within the heart.

5. Join 4 pieced units as shown to complete a Broken Dishes block.

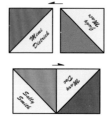 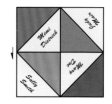

Make 20.

Quilt Assembly

1. Arrange the Broken Dishes blocks as shown. Sew the blocks together to form rows. Join the rows.

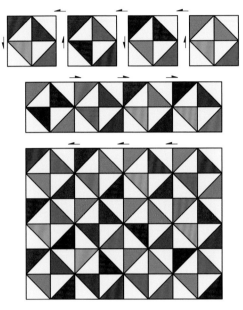

2. Sew the 1½"x 35½" inner border strips to opposite long sides of the quilt top. Sew the 1½" x 30½" inner border strips to the top and bottom edges of the quilt top.

3. Sew 4" x 37½" outer border strips to opposite long sides of the quilt top. Sew 4" x 37½" outer border strips to the top and bottom edges of the quilt top.

Finishing

1. Layer the quilt top with batting and backing; baste.

2. Quilt in-the-ditch around the squares, triangles, and on either side of the purple border strips. Free-motion quilt in the border. Use metallic thread to add sparkle to the jewel-tone prints. If desired, quilt hearts in the off-white triangles.

3. Bind the edges with the 2"-wide pink strips.

4. Add a label to the back of your quilt.

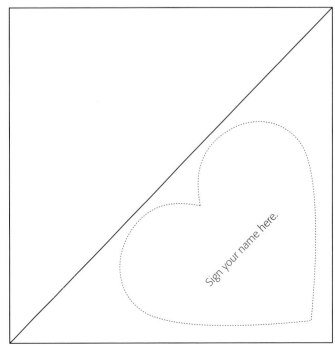

Sign your name here.

GROUP PROJECT

MAKE KITS BY placing a personalized copy of the letter★ below, 2 jewel-tone squares, 2 off-white squares, and a self-addressed-stamped envelope in a plastic zipper-lock bag.

Dear Friend,

When things go wrong, wouldn't we all like to throw dishes against a brick wall? Quilters can help by piecing these 5" squares into "Broken Dishes" blocks for _____ .

INSTRUCTIONS

1. Place the off-white squares on top of the jewel-tone squares, right sides together. Use a pencil and ruler to draw a diagonal line on the off-white squares. Draw a line ¼" on either side of the center line.
2. Sew on the ¼" lines. Cut on the marked center diagonal line. Press the seams toward the dark fabrics. You have just made 4 pieced units!
3. Sign your name or write a personal message on the off-white side of the squares with a fine-line permanent pen. Place the square on top of the full-size drawing and try to keep your name within the heart. The blocks will be trimmed a little smaller for the quilt.
4. This completes 4 pieced squares. Do not sew them together.
5. Please mail them back to _____ by _____ . If you have any questions, my phone number is _____ . *(name)*   *(date)*

Thank you very much!

_____

(Signature)

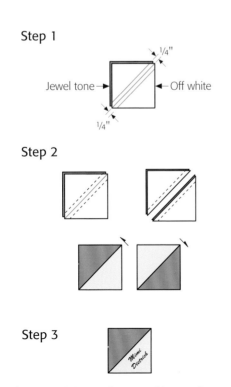

Step 1

Jewel tone → □ ← Off white

¼"

¼"

Step 2

Step 3

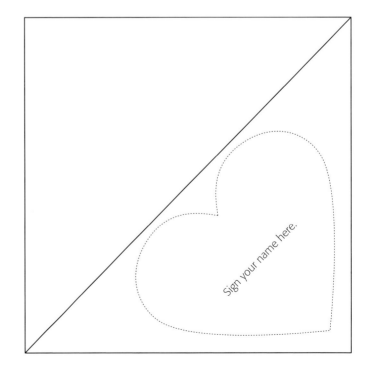

Sign your name here.

★*You have permission to photocopy this page for personal use.*

ORGANIZATIONS

RGANIZATIONS DEDICATED TO breast-cancer awareness and research provide valuable information. The American Cancer Society provides literature about breast cancer and refers patients to support groups. Reach to Recovery is a program operated by volunteers who have been mastectomy patients. They provide emotional support and helpful hints as they visit patients after surgery. Y-ME matches newly diagnosed women with volunteers who are breast-cancer survivors.

The Susan G. Komen Breast Cancer Foundation is one of the largest private funders of research in the United States dedicated solely to breast cancer. This foundation organizes Komen Race for the Cure® events, fund-raisers held annually in many cities throughout the U.S., and provides funds for research, education, screening, and treatment. I have walked in the Baltimore race for the past three years and it is a very moving experience. At the end of the race, they photograph all the survivors so that other racers go home with a positive feeling about their contributions. It is overwhelming to see so many people who have survived this disease.

Komen Race for the Cure® survivors, Baltimore, Maryland, 1998.

The Baltimore Affiliate of the Komen Foundation also sponsors a spring seminar in Baltimore, where health-care professionals and survivors present educational information. This well-attended event lets us know we are not alone.

Quilters have raised money for mammograms by responding to the "Yes Mam!" Challenge announced in 1990 at Quilt America. Since that time, "Yes Mam!" has raised over $100,000 from fund-raising quilts, grants, and donations. They challenge quilters to make quilts and donate the proceeds to a facility in their home community to provide free or at-cost mammograms for underinsured women. It involves purchasing a kit, and the kit proceeds fund a permanent project at Indianapolis-area imaging facilities. Additionally, these quilters are invited to a competition at Quilt America, where awards in the amount of $500, $250, and $100 are given to the top three quilts.

Quilters can also buy "Quilt for a Cure" fabrics, a collection designed by Bonnie Benn Stratton for Northcott-Monarch and Hi-Fashion Fabrics, Inc. A portion of the purchase price of every yard of fabric in the collection is donated to the Breast Cancer Research Foundation, founded by Evelyn Lauder. Look for special "Quilt for a Cure" tags on bolts of fabric. All of these organizations are "blossoms of hope" in the fight against breast cancer.

Blossoms of Hope

Blossoms of Hope by Mimi Dietrich, 1999, Baltimore, Maryland, 34" x 34"; quilted by Mimi Dietrich. Dogwood blossoms symbolizing "love in adversity" are appliquéd on a background fabric printed with white-on-white ribbons. The appliqué fabrics were chosen to match the dogwood flowers printed on the border fabric. Shopping for the perfect fabric is part of the fun of quilting!

Materials

(42"-wide fabric)

- ⅜ yd. white-on-white print for appliqué background squares
- 1 yd. floral print for setting pieces and outer borders
- ⅜ yd. light pink print for appliqué pieces and inner borders
- ⅜ yd. green print for appliqué pieces and binding
- Scrap of dark pink print for appliqué pieces
- Scrap of gold print for appliqué pieces
- 1⅛ yds. for backing
- 38" x 38" batting

Cutting

From the white-on-white print, cut:

- 4 squares, each 9½" x 9½", for background squares

From the floral print, cut:

- 1 square, 9½" x 9½", for setting square
- 1 square, 14" x 14"; cut square twice diagonally for a total of 4 side setting triangles
- 2 squares, each 7¼" x 7¼"; cut squares once diagonally for a total of 4 corner setting triangles
- 2 strips, each 3½" x 28", for outer side borders
- 2 strips, each 3½" x 34", for outer top and bottom borders

From the light pink print, cut:

- 2 strips, each 1½" x 26", for inner side borders
- 2 strips, each 1½" x 28," for inner top and bottom borders
- 16 of template 1 for heart shape

From the green print, cut:

- 4 strips, each 2" x 40", for binding
- 16 of template 4 for leaves

From the dark pink print, cut:

- 16 of template 2 for "teardrops"

From the gold print, cut:

- 4 of template 3 for center circles

Block Assembly

FINISHED SIZE: 9"

1. Center the 9½" background square on the full-size appliqué pattern on page 62 and trace the appliqué design.

2. Appliqué the heart-shaped petals, letting the center edges lie flat over the placement lines for the center circle.

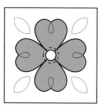

3. Appliqué the "teardrops" at the outer edges of the petals.

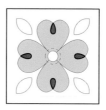

4. Appliqué the center circle and the leaves.

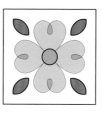

Make 4.

60

Quilt Assembly

1. Arrange the Blossoms of Hope blocks, setting square, and side setting triangles as shown. Sew the blocks and triangles together to form diagonal rows.

2. Join the rows, adding the corner setting triangles last.

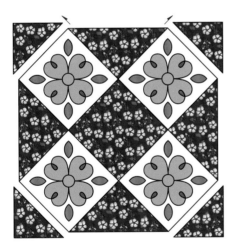

3. Sew the 1½" x 26" inner border strips to opposite sides of the quilt top. Sew the 1½" x 28" inner border strips to the top and bottom edges of the quilt top.

4. Sew the 3½" x 28" outer border strips to opposite sides of the quilt top. Sew the 3½" x 34" outer border strips to the top and bottom edges of the quilt top.

Finishing

1. Layer the quilt top with batting and backing; baste.

2. Outline-quilt around the appliquéd blossoms and the background squares. Quilt in-the-ditch around the leaves, teardrops, and on each side of the inner border. Quilt around the flowers on the printed fabric.

3. Bind the edges with the 2"-wide green print strips.

4. Add a label to the back of your quilt.

VOLUNTEERS

❧

THE GREAT AMERICAN Quilters in Severna Park, Maryland, devote some of their quilting time and energy to support cancer awareness and research. An early group project was to put together quilt blocks for a member whose husband had cancer—a quilt for him, another for her. In their journal they write that they "envision each of those plaid squares as a prayer sent heavenward each time they nestle under their colors."

For the past two years, the Great American Quilters made a quilt to raffle at the Relay for Life, where their team participated in a 24-hour event: walking, running, laughing, eating, and of course, quilting. They designed T-shirts, made a banner, and participated with a slogan: Piecing Our Hearts Together for a Cure. They donated a heart quilt to the American Cancer Society in memory of their friend's husband, and raised over $4500 the first year. As they made the quilt, they "laughed together, cried together, and lost sleep together. We truly got to know each other." Their quilt became a "legacy to the celebration of life and to the hope of finding a cure." The following Great American Quilters made "Forget-me-nots" as their Relay for Life quilt for the year 2000: Pat Anderson, Teri Baca, Paddy Bates, Joyce Burns, Robin Doane, Julie Doherty, Ruth Tallman, Robin Lukens, Peggy O'Berry, Jeanette Perry, Mary Lou Pfeifer, Sue Pivec, Debbie Westlund, and Linda Newsom.

Forget-me-nots

Forget-me-nots by Mimi Dietrich, stitched by the Great American Quilters, Pat Anderson, Teri Baca, Paddy Bates, Joyce Burns, Robin Doane, Julie Doherty, Ruth Tallman, Robin Lukens, Peggy O'Berry, Jeanette Perry, Mary Lou Pfeifer, Sue Pivec, Debbie Westlund, 1999, Severna Park, Maryland, 72" x 89"; quilted by Linda Newsom. Pink-and-white Rail Fence blocks produce ribbons that connect the forget-me-not flowers made from Nine Patch blocks.

Materials
(42"-wide fabric)

- 3¼ yds. white print for Rail Fence blocks, setting squares, and side setting triangles
- 2⅜ yds. pink print for Rail Fence blocks and inner border
- 1¼ yds. dark blue print for Nine Patch blocks and binding
- ¾ yd. green print for Nine Patch blocks
- ¼ yd. gold print for Nine Patch blocks
- 2½ yds. blue print for outer border
- 5½ yds. for backing
- 76" x 93" batting
- 32 gold ⅞" plastic buttons

Cutting

From the white print, cut:
- 16 strips, each 2½" x 40", for Rail Fence blocks
- 6 strips, each 6½" x 40"; crosscut strips into a total of 31 squares, each 6½" x 6½", for setting squares
- 2 strips, each 9¾" x 40"; crosscut strips into a total of 7 squares, each 9¾" x 9¾"; cut squares twice diagonally for a total of 28 side setting triangles
- 2 squares, each 5⅛" x 5⅛"; cut squares once diagonally for a total of 4 corner setting triangles

From the pink print, cut the following strips on the lengthwise grain:
- 8 strips, each 2½" x 40", for Rail Fence blocks
- 2 strips, each 2½" x 77", for inner side borders
- 2 strips, each 2½" x 64", for inner top and bottom borders

From the dark blue print, cut:
- 8 strips, each 2½" x 40", for Nine Patch blocks
- 9 strips, each 2" x 40", for binding

From the green print, cut:
- 8 strips, each 2½" x 40", for Nine Patch blocks

From the gold print, cut:
- 2 strips, each 2½" x 40", for Nine Patch blocks

From the blue print, cut the following strips on the lengthwise grain:
- 2 strips, each 4½" x 81", for outer side borders
- 2 strips, each 4½" x 72", for outer top and bottom borders

Rail Fence Blocks

FINISHED SIZE: 6"

Sew a 2½"-wide white strip to each long edge of a 2½"-wide pink strip. Make 8 strip sets. Use a ruler and rotary cutter to clean-cut the edges of the strip sets. Cut a total of 48 segments, each 6½" wide, to make the blocks.

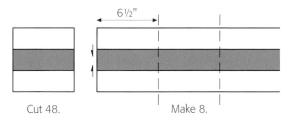

Cut 48.   Make 8.

Nine Patch Blocks

FINISHED SIZE: 6"

1. Sew a 2½"-wide green strip to each long edge of a 2½"-wide dark blue strip. Make 4 strip sets. Use a ruler and rotary cutter to clean-cut the edges of the strip sets. Cut a total of 64 segments, each 2½" wide.

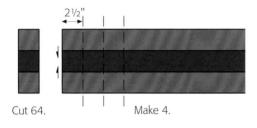

Cut 64.   Make 4.

2. Sew a 2½"-wide dark blue strip to each long edge of a 2½"-wide gold strip. Make 2 strip sets. Use a ruler and rotary cutter to clean-cut the edges of the strip sets. Cut a total of 32 segments, each 2½" wide.

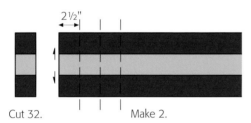

Cut 32.   Make 2.

3. Join 2 segments from step 1 and 1 segment from step 2 to complete a Nine Patch block.

Make 32.

Quilt Assembly

1. Arrange the Nine Patch blocks, Rail Fence blocks, setting squares, and side setting triangles as shown. Sew the blocks and triangles together to form diagonal rows.

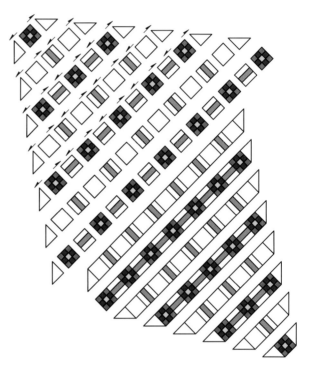

2. Join the rows, adding the corner setting triangles last.

3. Sew the 2½" x 77" inner border strips to opposite long sides of the quilt top. Sew the 2½" x 64" inner border strips to the top and bottom edges of the quilt top.

4. Sew the 4½" x 81" outer border strips to opposite long sides of the quilt top. Sew the 4½" x 72" outer border strips to the top and bottom edges of the quilt top.

1. Layer the quilt top with batting and backing; baste.

2. Quilt in-the-ditch around the Nine Patch blocks, Rail Fence blocks, and on either side of the inner borders. Refer to the diagram for quilting the flowers. Free-motion quilt around the flowers and in the border.

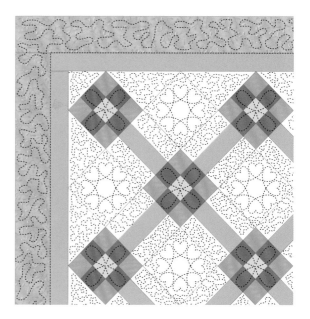

3. Bind the edges with the 2"-wide dark blue strips.

4. Add a label to the back of your quilt.

5. Sew the ⅞" gold buttons to the center of the gold squares in the Nine Patch blocks.

MEMORIES

THE INTENT OF THIS book is to present a positive outlook for breast-cancer survival and to use quilting as a tangible expression of caring feelings. Quilters are truly comforters when they use their stitches as a reminder of love and friendship.

It is a fact of life, however, that not everyone survives breast cancer. If someone loses the battle, consider using these quilt patterns to celebrate her life. Use her favorite colors and designs to capture her memory. Use the scrappy designs to patch together fabric from her clothing for a little quilt for her family. Make a quilt to donate in her honor for cancer research.

Let your tears fall while you stitch—but then smile as you remember the good times of her life!

Forget-me-nots Wall Hanging

Forget-me-nots Wall Hanging by Mimi Dietrich, 1999, Baltimore, Maryland, 34½" x 43"; quilted by Linda Newsom. Color placement in these traditional Nine Patch and Snowball blocks creates flowers and ribbons. The ribbon theme is repeated in the multicolored background fabric.

Materials

(42"-wide fabric)

- 1¼ yds. pastel print for Snowball blocks and setting triangles
- ¾ yd. pink print for Snowball blocks and Nine Patch blocks
- ⅝ yd. light blue print for Nine Patch blocks and binding
- ⅛ yd. yellow print for Nine Patch blocks
- 1⅜ yds. for backing
- 39" x 47" batting

Cutting

From the pastel print, cut:

- 4 strips, each 6½" x 40"; crosscut strips into a total of 20 squares, each 6½" x 6½", for Snowball blocks
- 4 squares, each 9¾" x 9¾"; cut squares twice diagonally for a total of 16 side setting triangles (you will have 2 extra triangles)
- 2 squares, each 5⅛" x 5⅛"; cut squares once diagonally for a total of 4 corner setting triangles

From the pink print, cut:

- 4 strips, each 2½" x 40", for Nine Patch blocks
- 5 strips, each 2½" x 40"; crosscut strips into a total of 62 squares, each 2½" x 2½", for Snowball blocks

From the light blue print, cut:

- 4 strips, each 2½" x 40", for Nine Patch blocks
- 4 strips, each 2" x 40", for binding

From the yellow print, cut:

- 1 strip, 2½" x 40", for Nine Patch blocks

Snowball Blocks

FINISHED SIZE: 6"

1. Using a pencil, draw a diagonal line on the wrong side of each 2½" pink print square.

2. Place a 2½" pink square on the corner of a 6½" pastel print square as shown. Sew on the line. Trim away the outer fabric ¼" from the stitching line. Press the triangle toward the corner.

3. Add corners as shown to make the following Snowball blocks.

Make 6.   Make 10.   Make 4.

Nine Patch Blocks

FINISHED SIZE: 6"

1. Sew a 2½"-wide pink strip to each long edge of a 2½"-wide blue strip. Make 2 strip sets. Use a ruler and rotary cutter to clean-cut the edges of the strip sets. Cut a total of 24 segments, each 2½" wide.

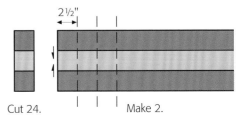

Cut 24.   Make 2.

2. Sew a 2½"-wide blue strip to each long edge of a 2½"-wide yellow strip. Make 1 strip set. Use a ruler and rotary cutter to clean-cut the edges of the strip set. Cut a total of 12 segments, each 2½" wide.

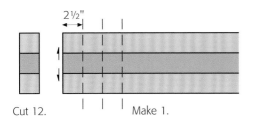

Cut 12.   Make 1.

3. Join 2 segments from step 1 and 1 segment from step 2 to complete a Nine Patch block.

Make 12.

Quilt Assembly

1. Arrange the Nine Patch blocks, Snowball blocks, and side setting triangles as shown. Sew the blocks and triangles together to form diagonal rows.

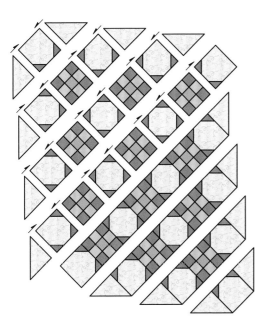

2. Join the rows, adding the corner setting triangles last.

Finishing

1. Layer the quilt top with batting and backing; baste.

2. Outline-quilt in the pink "ribbons." Refer to the diagram for quilting the flowers. Free-motion quilt in the background areas.

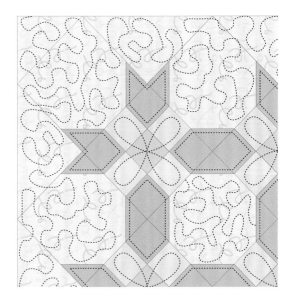

3. Bind the edges with the 2"-wide blue strips.

4. Add a label to the back of your quilt.

Basic Quiltmaking Techniques

ROTARY CUTTING

THE PIECES FOR the quilts in this book are cut with a rotary cutter, cutting mat, and acrylic ruler.

1. To straighten the fabric and prepare the fabric for cutting, fold the fabric in half lengthwise with the selvages parallel. If you prefer, bring the bottom fold up to meet the selvages for a shorter cutting distance.

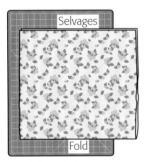
Fabric folded once

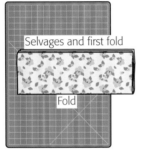
Fabric folded twice

2. Place the fabric on the cutting mat. Place a 6" square ruler on the fold nearest you, making sure it is aligned with the fold. Place a larger ruler (6" x 12" or 6" x 24") next to the square ruler so that it covers the uneven edges of the fabric.

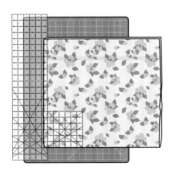
Align rulers.

3. Remove the 6" square ruler and make a clean cut along the edge of the larger ruler. Roll the rotary cutter away from you, using firm pressure.

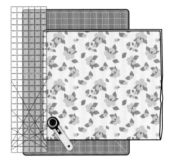
Make clean cut.

Cutting Strips

TO CUT STRIPS, align the clean-cut edge of the fabric with the desired ruler marking and cut.

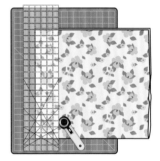

Cutting Squares

TO CUT SQUARES, cut a strip the desired measurement; then crosscut the strip into squares.

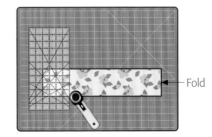
Fold

Cutting Triangles

TO CUT 2 triangles from a square, cut a square the desired measurement. Place the ruler diagonally across the square and cut the square into 2 triangles.

To cut 4 triangles from a square, cut a square the desired measurement. Cut the square twice diagonally for a total of 4 triangles.

MACHINE PIECING

MANY QUILTERS USE a sewing machine to sew patchwork, to join hand-appliquéd blocks, or to attach borders.

Sewing a ¼" Seam Allowance

THE PRESSER FOOT on your sewing machine is your sewing guide for machine piecing. Many machines have a presser foot that measures ¼" from the stitching line to the right edge of the foot.

To test your sewing guide, sew a sample seam, guiding the cut edge of your fabric just under the right-hand edge of the foot. Measure the resulting seam allowance and adjust, if necessary, so your seams will measure ¼". You can also place a piece of masking tape on your machine to mark the ¼" seam allowance.

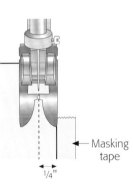

Masking tape

¼"

Sewing the Pieces Together

SEWING PATCHWORK PIECES on the machine can be fun and fast if you chain-piece the patches as you sew. Start by sewing the first patch. Sew from cut edge to cut edge, using a small stitch length (12 to 15 stitches per inch). At the end of the seam, stop sewing, but don't cut the thread. Take the next set of patches and feed it into the machine right after the first one. Continue feeding pieces without cutting the thread. When all of your pieces have been sewn, clip the thread between the pieces. No wasted thread tails to throw away!

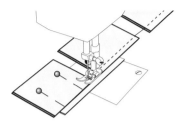

MAKING APPLIQUÉ QUILTS

INSTEAD OF PIECING fabrics together to make patchwork patterns, fabrics can be applied (appliquéd) on top of other fabrics. Curved designs can easily be accomplished with appliqué.

Background Fabric

THE BACKGROUND FABRIC for appliqué is usually cut in a square. If the finished size of an appliqué block is 9" square, cut a 9½" square to allow for seam allowances. Sometimes it is better to cut the square an inch larger to start, then trim it to the correct size after the appliqué has been completed. Cut background squares with a large square acrylic ruler and a rotary cutter.

To place the appliqué pieces on the background fabric accurately, you'll need to mark the design on the fabric. If your background fabric is white or off-white, it's easy to trace the design onto the fabric. Just place the fabric, right side up, over the pattern so that the design is centered. Trace the design carefully. I like to use a silver marking pencil to trace the design. The marks will be dark enough and will wash out after the quilt is completed.

If your background fabric is dark, use a light box or tape the pattern and fabric to a window on a sunny day. Trace the design with a white chalk marker.

Preparing Appliqués

BEFORE SEWING THE appliqué fabrics to the background fabric, they should be prepared so that the seam allowances are turned under smoothly. This will help you place the appliqués accurately on the marked background fabric. Use freezer-paper templates to make perfectly shaped appliqués.

Freezer–Paper Appliqué

1. Place the freezer paper, plastic-coated side down, on your pattern and trace the design with a sharp pencil. With repeated designs, such as the rose and leaves, make a plastic template and trace around it onto the freezer paper.

2. Cut out the freezer-paper shape on the pencil line. Do not add seam allowances.

3. Place the plastic-coated side of the freezer paper against the wrong side of the appliqué fabric. Iron the freezer paper to the wrong side of the appliqué fabric. Use a dry, hot iron.

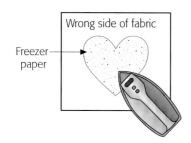

Wrong side of fabric

Freezer paper

4. Cut out the appliqué shape, adding a ¼"-wide seam allowance around the outside of the freezer paper.

5. Baste the seam allowance over the freezer-paper edges. Clip any inside points, and fold outside points.

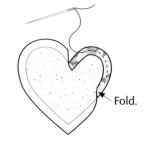

Fold.

6. Pin or baste the appliqué to the background fabric.

7. Stitch the appliqué to the background fabric using the Traditional Appliqué Stitch (directions at right).

8. After the shape has been appliquéd, remove the basting stitches. Cut a small slit in the background fabric behind the appliqué and remove the freezer paper with tweezers.

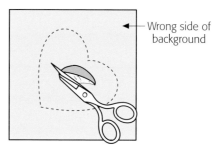

Wrong side of background

9. Press the appliqué from the wrong side.

Traditional Appliqué Stitch

The traditional appliqué stitch is appropriate for sewing all areas of appliqué designs, including sharp points and curves.

1. Start with a single strand of thread approximately 18" long and tie a knot in one end.

To hide your knot when you start, slip your needle into the seam allowance from the wrong side of the appliqué piece, bringing it out along the fold line. The knot will be hidden inside the seam allowance.

2. Stitch along the top edge of the appliqué. If you are right-handed, stitch from right to left. If you are left-handed, stitch from left to right. Start the first stitch by moving your needle straight off the appliqué, inserting the needle into the background fabric.

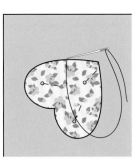

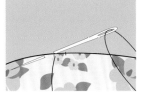

Let the needle travel under the background fabric parallel to the edge of the appliqué, bringing it up about ⅛" away along the pattern line. As you bring the needle back up, pierce the edge of the appliqué piece, catching only one or two threads of the folded edge.

3. Move the needle straight off the appliqué into the background fabric. Let your needle travel under the background, bringing it up about ⅛" away, again catching the edge of the appliqué. Give the thread a slight tug and continue stitching. The only visible parts of the stitch are very small dots of thread along the appliqué edge.

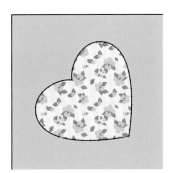

The part of the stitch that travels forward will be seen as ⅛" stitches on the wrong side of the background fabric. The length of your stitches should be consistent as you stitch along the straight edges. Smaller stitches are sometimes necessary for curves and points.

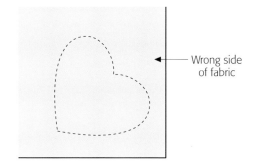

Wrong side of fabric

SQUARING UP BLOCKS

BEFORE YOU STITCH your blocks together to assemble your quilt, it is sometimes necessary to "square up" your blocks. Trim the edges using an acrylic ruler and rotary cutter. Be sure to leave a ¼" seam allowance beyond any points or other important block details near the outside edges of your blocks.

If you cut appliqué blocks larger than necessary, trim the blocks square. Use a large square acrylic ruler or cut a square of template plastic the correct size. Draw around the edges of the plastic to indicate the size, then cut with scissors or a rotary cutter.

ADDING BORDERS

WHEN THE PATCHWORK has been completed and the quilt blocks have been stitched together, borders add a finishing frame to your design.

Straight-Cut Borders

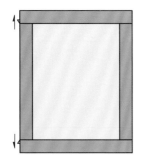

To make straight-cut borders, two of the borders are cut the size of the inner patchwork design, and the other two borders are cut longer, the length of the total design.

If you are making a large quilt or a quilt with many patchwork pieces, the size of the quilt may vary because everyone pieces a little differently. For this reason, it's always a good idea to cut the borders to match the actual measurements of your quilt. Measuring through the center of the quilt top is more accurate because sometimes the edges may stretch. This also helps avoid stretched and rippled borders.

1. Measure the quilt through the center of the patchwork. Cut 2 border strips to match the measurement. Fold each border in half and mark with a straight pin. Fold each quilt edge in half and mark with a pin.

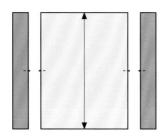

Measure center of quilt, top to bottom.

2. Starting with the sides, pin the side borders to the quilt top, matching the center pins and ends. Ease the edge of the quilt to fit the borders if necessary. Sew from edge to edge using a ¼"-wide seam allowance. Press seams toward the border, or toward the darker fabric when adding more than one border.

3. Now measure through the center for the top and bottom borders. Cut 2 border strips to match the measurement. Mark the center of the borders and quilt edges; pin and stitch. Press the seams in the same direction as the first borders.

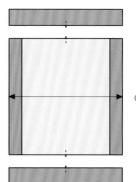

Measure center of quilt, side to side, including borders.

MARKING THE QUILTING LINES

QUILTING LINES CAN follow the lines of patchwork in the quilt, outline appliqué designs, or embellish spaces between the designs. Mark the quilting lines before basting the three layers together. If the quilt lies flat during the marking process, lines will be smooth and accurate.

There are several tools used to mark quilting designs on the quilt top. You can use a regular pencil (#2 or #3), a fine-lead mechanical pencil, a silver marking pencil, or a chalk pencil or chalk marker for dark fabrics. A water-erasable marker can be used to mark the quilting designs, but may disappear before the quilting is completed if the weather is humid. Whichever tool you use for marking, test the tool on a sample of your fabric before using it on your quilt. Make sure you can see the lines, and make sure you can remove them.

To mark straight lines, use a yardstick or a long acrylic ruler. Parallel lines on acrylic rulers help keep the lines even. You can also use masking tape to mark straight lines.

To mark more elaborate quilting designs, place the quilt top on top of the design and trace the design onto the fabric. Use a light box or tape your work against a bright window if you have trouble seeing the design through the fabric. Many precut plastic quilting stencils are available in quilt shops.

It may not be necessary to mark quilting designs if you are planning to quilt in-the-ditch next to seams or if you are outlining patchwork pieces.

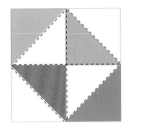

Quilt in-the-Ditch

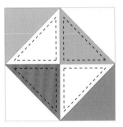

Outline Quilt

BASTING THE THREE QUILT LAYERS

BEFORE YOU BEGIN to quilt, you must baste together the quilt top, batting, and backing. This secures the three layers and keeps the fabrics from slipping.

1. Press the quilt backing so that it is smooth. Cut the backing at least 2" larger than the quilt top all the way around.

2. Place the backing on a smooth surface, right side down. Use masking tape to fasten the corners and sides to the surface.

3. Place the batting on the backing, smoothing it out carefully. If it is very wrinkled, let it relax overnight before you layer the quilt.

4. Lay the quilt top, right side up, on the batting. Pin the layers together in several places.

5. If you plan to hand quilt, use a long needle and light-colored basting thread. Start in the center and baste a large X in the center of the quilt, then baste parallel lines to hold the layers together. The lines should be 4" to 6" apart. The more rows of basting you have, the better your layers will stay together. Baste around the outside edges.

If you plan to machine quilt, use safety pins to baste the layers together.

QUILTING
Hand Quilting

HAND-QUILTING STITCHES are short running stitches used to sew the top, batting, and backing of your quilt together.

1. To begin quilting, tie a single knot in the end of an 18" length of quilting thread. Insert the needle through the top layer of the quilt about ¾" from the point where you want to start stitching. Slide the needle through the batting layer and bring the needle out at the starting point.

2. Gently tug on the thread until the knot pops through the fabric and is buried in the

batting. Take a backstitch and begin quilting, making a small running stitch that goes through all layers. Take two, three, or four stitches at a time, trying to keep them straight and even.

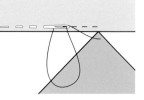

3. To end a line of quilting, make a single knot approximately ¼" from your quilt top. Take one more backstitch into your quilt, tugging the knot into the batting layer and bringing the needle out ¾" away from your stitches. Clip the thread and let the end disappear into your quilt.

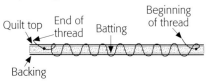

Machine Quilting

QUILTS MAY BE quilted quickly by machine. It helps to make sure your machine is oiled and in good working order. Adjust your stitch length so that it is a little longer than normal, approximately 10 stitches per inch. Test your machine to make sure that the thread tension is even on the top and bottom.

Straight-Line Quilting

Use a "walking foot" or "even-feed" foot on your machine to stitch straight lines, outline borders, or quilt in-the-ditch. A walking foot helps to ease the quilt layers through the machine, creating straight lines without puckering.

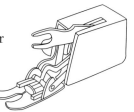

Walking or even-feed foot

Free-Motion Quilting

Free-motion quilting is used to fill in areas or to embellish spaces between patchwork designs. Use this technique to outline-quilt a motif or flower in the fabric, to stipple quilt, or meander around areas in the quilt. You can also quilt ribbon designs on the quilt using free-motion quilting.

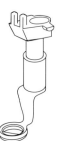

Darning Foot

Use a "darning foot" and lower the feed dogs on your

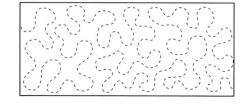

machine so you can move the fabric in any direction. This technique takes practice or may require a little warm-up time on a sample before you actually sew on your quilt.

BINDING

BINDING ADDS THE finishing touch to your quilt. It is usually a good idea to use one of your darker fabrics to frame the design.

1. Baste around the edge of the quilt to securely hold the three layers together. Trim any excess threads, batting, or backing even with the front of the quilt.

2. Measure the distance around the quilt and add 10". Cut enough 2"-wide strips of binding fabric across the 42" width of fabric to equal this measurement. These can be cut quickly with a rotary cutter and a clear acrylic ruler.

3. Sew the strips together, using diagonal seams, to create one long strip of binding. To make diagonal seams, cross two strip ends at right angles, right sides together. Draw a line across the pieces, then sew on

the line. Your seam will be exact, and you can unfold a continuous strip.

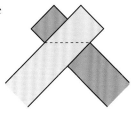

Trim the excess fabric, leaving a ¼"-wide seam allowance.

Press this seam open to distribute the thickness of the seam.

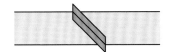

4. Fold the binding strip in half lengthwise, wrong sides together, and press with a hot steam iron.

5. Starting 6" from the corner, align the raw edges of the binding with the raw edges of the quilt. Start sewing approximately 4" from the end of the binding, using a ¼"-wide seam. For durability, sew this seam by machine.

6"

6. To miter the corners of the binding, stop stitching ¼" from the corner and backstitch.

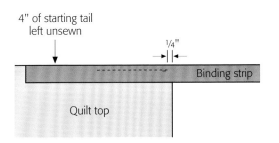

4" of starting tail left unsewn

¼"

Binding strip

Quilt top

Fold the binding diagonally as shown, so that it extends straight up from the second edge of the quilt.

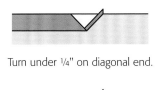

Quilt top

Then, fold the binding down even with the second edge of the quilt. The fold should be even with the first edge. Start sewing the binding ¼" from the fold, making sure to backstitch. Repeat for the remaining corners.

Fold.

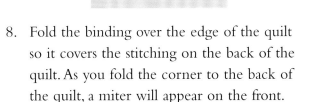

Quilt top

7. To connect the ends of the binding, allow the end to overlap the beginning edge by 2". Cut the end diagonally, with the shortest end of the diagonal on top, nearest to you. Turn the diagonal edge under ¼" and insert the beginning "tail" inside the diagonal fold. Continue sewing the binding onto the quilt.

Turn under ¼" on diagonal end.

8. Fold the binding over the edge of the quilt so it covers the stitching on the back of the quilt. As you fold the corner to the back of the quilt, a miter will appear on the front.

On the back, fold one side first, then the other, to create a miter on the back.

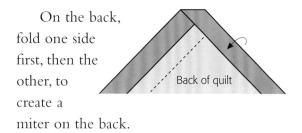

9. Hand stitch the binding to the back of the quilt, using the traditional appliqué stitch. Hand stitch the diagonal fold.

MAKING A LABEL FOR YOUR QUILT

YOU HAVE MADE a very special quilt. Make a label for the back of your quilt and sign your name and date. You may also want to include information about the quilt: a dedication, group information, or a story about your quilt.

Resources

"Yes Mam!"®
    Quilt America
    2217 Avalon Court
    Kokomo, IN 46902-3101

American Cancer Society
    1-800-ACS-2345
    www.cancer.org

The Susan G. Komen Breast Cancer Foundation
    1-800 I'M AWARE
    www.breastcancerinfo.com

The Cancer Information Center
    Toll Free: 1-800-4-CANCER
    www.nci.nih.gov

Y-ME National Breast Cancer Organization
    1-800-221-2141
    www.y-me.org

National Alliance of Breast Cancer Organizations
    1-888-806-2226
    www.nabco.org

"Quilt for a Cure"™
    Merryvale, Ltd.
    11416 Vale Road
    Oakton, VA 22124
    1-703-264-8959

Pleasant Company
    (for doll hangers)
    1-800-845-0005
    www.americangirl.com

Michell Marketing, Inc.
    (for 6" dark gray hangers with hook top
    and heart center)
    770-458-6500